GREAT QUOTES
TO INSPIRE
GREAT TEACHERS

*T*hings that upset us
often inspire us.
Things that disturb us
often teach us.
Discomfort often leads
to discovery.

—*Noah benShea*

*A*bove all
we take pride
in the education
of our children.

—*Josephus*

GREAT QUOTES
TO INSPIRE
GREAT TEACHERS

Noah benShea

Skyhorse Publishing

Skyhorse Publishing books may be purchased in bulk at special discounts for sales promotion, corporate gifts, fund-raising, or educational purposes. Special editions can also be created to specifications. For details, contact the Special Sales Department, Skyhorse Publishing, 307 West 36th Street, 11th Floor, New York, NY 10018 or info@skyhorsepublishing.com.

Skyhorse® and Skyhorse Publishing® are registered trademarks of Skyhorse Publishing, Inc.®, a Delaware corporation.

Visit our website at www.skyhorsepublishing.com.

10 9 8 7 6 5 4 3 2 1

Library of Congress Cataloging-in-Publication Data is available on file.

Cover design and photo credit Tracy E. Miller

Print ISBN: 978-1-62914-689-8
Ebook ISBN: 978-1-62914-969-1

Printed in the United States of America

CONTENTS

FOREWORD

The poet Robert Browning refers to inspiration as "the splendor of a sudden thought." But whether it is the splendor of a sudden thought or the transforming glory of a personal epiphany, it is a rare soul who becomes a teacher who has not been smitten by inspiration and the thought of similarly inspiring others. To this end, little helps great teachers make their point to a student like access to a great thought at the right moment. In that effort, this book is intended as an ally across time.

But there is more to this book. Though great teachers certainly do inspire, teaching is love twined with labor, and teachers themselves need inspiration. Hopefully the thoughts herein will also serve you so you may be of service. Each of us, in life and teaching, is the source of the other's river.

Teaching today is no less a challenge than it was yesterday and in many ways more. It challenges teachers intellectually, emotionally, spiritually, and physically. With this in mind, here are quotes that will help you translate the nature of today's challenge to others and to yourselves and perhaps remind every teacher that to relax after a day's teaching is appropriate emotional homework. Make no mistake this book is as much for you as for your students. Learning, like charity, begins at home.

The ideas in this book are culled from the centuries. They are timely and timeless just as great teachers are never out of date. You can open this book to any page and offer learning or find learning. In its own way, this book is designed to be a wise and gentle friend. Not unlike a teacher.

Finally, let me say that my heart goes out to teachers. This is not pathos but heartfelt respect. Any of us who have benefited from learning have benefited from teachers. To each of my teachers who cared and shared their learning with me, I say thank you. To those who time has taken, I say thank you through the veil of time. To you who read this book, I humbly dedicate this work.

— *Noah benShea*

ACKNOWLEDGMENTS

I wish to thank the following members of my research team for their invaluable help in making this book possible.

Director of Research
Ms. Jordan Arin benShea

Senior Research Staff
Ms. Claudia Castaneda
Mr. Luke Delgado
Mr. Matthew Miles
Ms. Anna Weichselbraun

Associate Research Staff
Mr. Michael Tinney
Ms. Holly Carlson
Ms. Sarah Dunlap

ABOUT THE AUTHOR

Noah benShea is a poet, philosopher, scholar, humorist, lecturer, and international best-selling author who was, by the age of 23, an Assistant Dean of Students at UCLA and, by 30, a consulting fellow to the esteemed Center for the Study of Democratic Institutions in Santa Barbara, California. His first book, a collection of poetry titled *Don't Call It Anything,* received the Schull Award from the Southern California Poetry Society. He has lectured at numerous universities, and has given a keynote address at the Library of Congress. His work has been included in publications of Oxford University and the World Bible Society in Jerusalem.

Often referred to as the guru's guru, Noah benShea is the author of eleven books, including the broadly loved *Jacob the Baker* series, which are translated around the world and embraced as timeless fables. His insightful perspective on life, *Noah's Window,* is carried globally via the Internet and has been enjoyed by countless readers for many years via the *New York Times* Newspaper Regional Network. His essays were nominated for a Pulitzer Prize in Journalism in 1997, and in 1999 he was nominated for the Grawemeyer Award for Ideas Improving the World. His most recent book, *Remember This My Children* is a collection of Mr. benShea's original thoughts twined with heart-touching photographs intended as a timeless legacy between parents and children. In addition to his reflective life, Mr. benShea was a founding partner and later chairman of a national manufacturing company, and he continues to serves as an advisor to North American business and community leaders. Born in Toronto, Mr. benShea is the father of two children and lives in Santa Barbara, California.

Mr. benShea may be contacted at www.noahswindow.com and/or noah@noahswindow.com

This book is dedicated to all the teachers who believed in us even when we believed they didn't know anything.

A teacher affects eternity.

—Henry B. Adams

THE ART OF TEACHING

Teaching is not a lost art,
but the regard for it
is a lost tradition.

—Jacques Barzun

*L*ittle warms us like the soul's own spark of self-worth.

—*Noah benShea*

⬚

*F*olks don't like to have somebody around knowin' more than they do. It aggravates 'em. You're not gonna change any of them by talkin' right, they've got to want to learn themselves, and when they don't want to learn there's nothing you can do but keep your mouth shut or talk their language.

—*Harper Lee*

⬚

*B*enevolence alone will not make a teacher, nor will learning alone do it. The gift of teaching is a peculiar talent, and implies a need and a craving in the teacher himself.

—*John Jay Chapman*

⬚

*W*hen will the public cease to insult the teacher's calling with empty flattery? When will men who would never for a moment encourage their own sons to enter the work of the public schools cease to tell us that education is the greatest and noblest of all human callings?

—*William C. Bagley*

*F*irst you destroy those who create values. Then you destroy those who know what the values are, and who also know that those destroyed before were in fact the creators of values. But real barbarism begins when no one can any longer judge or know that what he does is barbaric.

—*Ryszard Kapuscinski*

❈

*T*he cynic knows the price of everything
and the value of nothing.

—*Oscar Wilde*

❈

A teacher affects eternity; he can never tell
where his influence stops.

—*Henry B. Adams*

❈

*T*ry not to become a man of success,
but rather try to become a man of value.

—*Albert Einstein*

❈

*W*hat office is there which involves more responsibility,
which requires more qualifications, and which ought,
therefore, to be more honourable, than that of teaching?

—*Harriet Martineau*

*U*ntil you value yourself, you won't value your time.
Until you value your time, you will not
do anything with it.

—*M. Scott Peck*

▨

*H*ousework is a breeze. Cooking is a pleasant diversion.
Putting up a retaining wall is a lark. But teaching
is like climbing a mountain.

—*Fawn M. Brodie*

▨

*O*ne looks back with appreciation to the brilliant
teachers . . . with gratitude to those who
touched our human feeling . . .

—*Carl Gustav Jung*

▨

*K*nowing how things work is the basis for appreciation,
and is thus a source of civilized delight.

—*William Safire*

▨

*A*merica today is capable of terrific intolerance about
smoking, or toxic waste that threatens trout. But only a
deeply confused society is more concerned about
protecting lungs than minds.

—*Gary Wills*

There has never been another you. With no effort on
your part you were born to be something very special and
set apart. What you are going to do in appreciation
of that gift is a decision only you can make.

—*Dan Zadra*

❈

The ultimate value of life depends upon awareness,
and the power of contemplation
rather than upon mere survival.

—*Aristotle*

❈

It is the supreme art of the teacher to awaken joy
in creative expression and knowledge.

—*Albert Einstein*

❈

Nothing is intrinsically valuable; the value
of everything is attributed to it, assigned to it
from outside the thing itself, by people.

—*John Barth*

❈

I swear . . . to hold my teacher in this art equal to my
own parents; to make him partner in my livelihood; when
he is in need of money to share mine with him; to consider
his family as my own brothers and to teach them this art,
if they want to learn it, without fee or indenture.

—*Hippocrates*

$y$ou will be of as much value to others
as you have been to yourself.

—*Marcus Tullius Cicero*

❈

$\mathcal{W}$hen your values are clear to you,
making decisions becomes easier.

—*Roy Disney*

ADVERSITY

*C*omfort and prosperity
have never enriched
the world as much
as adversity has.

—*Billy Graham*

*W*e are all at risk at any moment
to be less than we might be. Knowing this
is the brother- and sisterhood of vulnerability.

—*Noah benShea*

❦

*E*ducation remains the key to both economic
and political empowerment.

—*Barbara Jordan*

❦

*H*old fast to dreams, for if dreams die,
life is a broken-winged bird that cannot fly.

—*Langston Hughes*

❦

*I*deologies separate us. Dreams and anguish
bring us together.

—*Eugene Ionesco*

❦

*G*o confidently in the direction of your dreams.
Live the life you have imagined.

—*Henry David Thoreau*

$\mathcal{T}$hrow your dreams into space like a kite,
and you do not know what it will bring back—
a new life, a new friend, a new country.

—*Anaïs Nin*

❧

$\mathcal{T}$here is no risk in dreaming.
To think of a life without risk is dreaming.

—*Noah benShea*

❧

$\mathcal{T}$he future belongs to those who believe
in the beauty of their dreams.

—*Eleanor Roosevelt*

❧

$\mathcal{D}$reams are the touchstones of our character.

—*Henry David Thoreau*

❧

$\mathcal{W}$e must learn to live together as brothers or
perish together as fools.

—*Martin Luther King, Jr.*

❧

$\mathcal{A}$merica's future will be determined by the home and
the school. The child becomes largely what he is taught;
hence we must watch what we teach, and how we live.

—*Jane Addams*

J had a terrible education. I attended a school
for emotionally disturbed teachers.

—*Woody Allen*

❧

*H*ow dare any parent or schoolteacher tell me
not to act colored.

—*Arna Bontemps*

❧

*I*t is difficult to understand precisely what the state
hopes to achieve by promoting the creation and
perpetuation of a subclass of illiterates within our
boundaries, surely adding to the problems and
costs of unemployment, welfare and crime.

—*William J. Brennan, Jr.*

❧

*I*n high school, I took a little English, some science, and
some hubcaps and some wheel covers.

—*Gates Brown*

❧

*T*he shrewd guess, the fertile hypothesis, the courageous
leap to a tentative conclusion—these are the most
valuable coin of the thinker at work. But in most
schools guessing is heavily penalized and is
associated somehow with laziness.

—*Jerome S. Bruner*

*W*e have to abandon the idea that schooling is
something restricted to youth. How can it be, in a world
where half the things a man knows at 20 are no longer
true at 40—and half the things he knows at 40
hadn't been discovered when he was 20?

—*Arthur C. Clarke*

🖋

*Y*ou don't develop courage by being happy in your
relationships every day. You develop it by surviving
difficult times and challenging adversity.

—*Barbara De Angelis*

🖋

*E*ducation is an ornament in prosperity
and a refuge in adversity.

—*Aristotle*

🖋

*R*ecommend virtue to your children, that alone—
not wealth—can give happiness.

—*Ludwig van Beethoven*

🖋

*A*dvise and counsel him; if he does not listen,
let adversity teach him.

—*Ethiopian proverb*

*A*dversity has the effect of eliciting talents, which in prosperous circumstances would have lain dormant.

—*Horace*

❧

*N*o one ever learned to run
who didn't first learn to stand on their own two feet.

—*Noah benShea*

❧

*S*he was a weak woman—too highly elated in prosperity,
too easily depressed by adversity—not considering
that both are situations of trial.

—*Sarah Josepha Hale*

❧

*W*eak minds sink under prosperity as well as adversity;
but strong and deep ones have two high tides.

—*David Hare*

❧

*E*very adversity, every failure, every heartache carries
with it the seed of an equal or greater benefit.

—*Napoleon Hill*

❧

*A*dversity reveals genius, prosperity conceals it.

—*Horace*

$\mathcal{B}$e willing to access joy in the face of adversity.

—C. W. *Metcalf*

❋

$\mathcal{I}$ would never have amounted to anything
were it not for adversity.

—J. C. *Penney*

❋

$\mathcal{L}$ife is never dull.
Use adversity as your sharpening stone.
Things don't have to be good for us to be great.

—*Noah benShea*

❋

$\mathcal{M}$any who seem to be struggling with adversity are
happy; many, amid great affluence, are utterly miserable.

—*Publius Cornelius Tacitus*

BEHAVIOR

$\mathcal{B}$ehavior is a mirror in
which everyone displays
his own image.

—*Johann Wolfgang Von Goethe*

*A*ctions don't speak louder than words. They shout.

—*Noah benShea*

◙

*A*lthough our inattention can contribute to our lack of total well-being, we also have the power to choose positive behaviors and responses. In that choice we change our every experience of life! Every thought, word, and behavior affects our greater health and well-being . . . physically, emotionally and spiritually.

—*Greg Anderson (US basketball player)*

◙

*M*orality cannot be legislated but behavior can be regulated. Judicial decrees may not change the heart, but they can restrain the heartless.

—*Martin Luther King, Jr.*

◙

*I*deological differences are no excuse for rudeness.

—*Judith Martin*

◙

*M*anners are socialized caring.

—*Noah benShea*

*O*nce you identify a period of life in which people get to stay out late but don't have to pay taxes—naturally, nobody wants to live any other way.

—*Judith Martin*

🐾

*T*oday's society will ignore almost any form of public behavior except getting in the express line with two extra items.

—*Paul Sweeney*

🐾

*T*he man of character, sensitive to the meaning of what he is doing, will know how to discover the ethical paths in the maze of possible behavior.

—*Earl Warren*

🐾

*T*he essence of good behavior is thinking about what's also good for others.

—*Noah benShea*

🐾

*A*n individual's self-concept is the core of his personality. It affects every aspect of human behavior: the ability to learn, the capacity to grow and change.

—*Joyce Brothers*

*D*on't confuse kindness with weakness.

—*Noah benShea*

❦

*Y*ou can't assume that kindness is an inherited trait. It is a learned behavior.

—*Katie Couric*

CHARACTER

No change of circumstances can repair a defect of character.

—*Ralph Waldo Emerson*

*C*haracter is less often something we grow into
and more often where we grow from.

—*Noah benShea*

⌘

*W*atch your thoughts; they become words.
Watch your words; they become actions.
Watch your actions; they become habits.
Watch your habits; they become character.
Watch your character; it becomes your destiny.

—*Frank Outlaw*

⌘

A man's character is his fate.

—*Heraclitus*

⌘

*E*ducation is when you read the fine print.
Experience is what you get if you don't.

—*Pete Seeger*

⌘

*F*ormal education will earn you a living,
self-education will make you a fortune.

—*Unknown*

I respect faith, but doubt is what gets you an education.
—*Wilson Mizner*

❧

*S*pend money to make character,
but don't spend character to make money.
—*Kashif Amin*

❧

*N*early all men can stand adversity, but if you want
to test a man's character, give him power.
—*Abraham Lincoln*

❧

*T*here is nothing in which people more betray
their character than in what they laugh at.
—*Johann Wolfgang Von Goethe*

❧

*I*t's really a wonder that I haven't dropped all my ideals,
because they seem so absurd and impossible to carry out.
Yet I keep them, because in spite of everything I still
believe that people are really good at heart.
—*Anne Frank*

*W*ho you are speaks so loudly I can't hear
what you're saying.

—*Ralph Waldo Emerson*

*O*ur character is what we do
when we think no one is looking.

—*H. Jackson Brown, Jr.*

*T*he true test of character is not how much we know how
to do, but how we behave when we don't know what to do.

—*John Holt*

*B*eing uptight does not necessarily mean
our character is upright.

—*Noah benShea*

*T*he measure of a man's real character is what he would
do if he knew he would never be found out.

—*Thomas B. Macaulay*

*W*hen you choose your friends, don't be short-changed
by choosing personality over character.

—*W. Somerset Maugham*

*T*he quality of strength lined with tenderness
is an unbeatable combination.

—*Maya Angelou*

❧

A college education should equip one to entertain three
things: a friend, an idea and oneself.

—*Thomas Ehrlich*

❧

*W*e're all actors who get better parts
when we work on our character.

—*Noah benShea*

❧

*E*ducation's purpose is to replace an empty mind
with an open one.

—*Malcolm Forbes*

❧

*C*haracter is the key to opening a closed mind.

—*Noah benShea*

❧

*E*ducation makes machines which act like men and
produces men who act like machines.

—*Erich Fromm*

*C*haracter is more than a good idea blossoming.
Character is the garden good ideas grow in.

—*Noah benShea*

⚜

*P*atience and tenacity of purpose are worth more than
twice their weight in cleverness.

—*Thomas Henry Huxley*

⚜

A clever character is not the same thing
as someone with character.

—*Noah benShea*

⚜

*T*he education of a man is never completed until he dies.

—*Robert E. Lee*

⚜

*D*uring my eighty-seven years, I have witnessed a whole
succession of technological revolutions. But none
of them has done away with the need for character
in the individual or the ability to think.

—*Bernard M. Baruch*

$\mathcal{T}$he best index to a person's character is (a) how he treats people who can't do him any good, and (b) how he treats people who can't fight back.

—*Abigail Van Buren*

🜨

$\mathcal{T}$he measure of a civilization is how people with power treat those without power.

—*Noah benShea*

🜨

$\mathcal{E}$very human being is intended to have a character of his own; to be what no others are, and to do what no other can do.

—*William Ellery Channing*

🜨

$\mathcal{T}$alent develops in tranquility, character in the full current of human life.

—*Johann Wolfgang Von Goethe*

🜨

$\mathcal{C}$haracter is what you know you are, not what others think you have.

—*Marva Collins*

*I*t takes a great deal of character strength to apologize
quickly out of one's heart rather than out of pity.
A person must possess himself and have a
deep sense of security in fundamental principles
and values in order to genuinely apologize.

—*Stephen R. Covey*

*C*haracter is not made in a crisis—it is only exhibited.

—*Robert Freeman*

*T*o keep your character intact you cannot stoop to filthy
acts. It makes it easier to stoop the next time.

—*Katharine Hepburn*

I look to a day when people will not be judged by the
color of their skin, but by the content of their character.

—*Martin Luther King Jr.*

*W*e should be too big to take offense
and too noble to give it.

—*Abraham Lincoln*

*G*ood character is more to be praised than outstanding
talent. Most talents are, to some extent, a gift. Good
character, by contrast, is not given to us. We have
to build it piece by piece, by thought, choice,
courage, and determination.

—*John Luther*

❈

*C*haracter consists of what you do
on the third and fourth tries.

—*James A. Michener*

❈

*I*t is with trifles and when he is off guard
that a man best reveals his character.

—*Arthur Schopenhauer*

❈

*C*haracter is always lost when a high ideal is sacrificed
on the altar of conformity and popularity.

—*Unknown*

❈

*C*haracter is a by-product; it is produced
in the great manufacture of daily duty.

—*Woodrow T. Wilson*

$\mathcal{M}$ercy to living beings, self restraint, truth, chastity
and contentment, right faith and knowledge, and
austerity are but the entourage of morality.

—*Sila-Prabhrita*

⊠

$\mathcal{W}$aste no more time arguing about
what a good man should be. Be one.

—*Marcus Aurelius*

⊠

$\mathcal{I}$f you pursue evil with pleasure, the pleasure passes away
and the evil remains. If you pursue good with labor,
the labor passes away but the good remains.

—*Marcus Tullius Cicero*

⊠

$\mathcal{I}$f there is righteousness in the heart, there will
be beauty in character.

—*Unknown*

CHILDREN

Tell me and I forget.
Show me and I remember.
Involve me
and I understand.

—Chinese proverb

*Y*ou can give children advice,
and they can give it back to you.

—*Noah benShea*

❧

*C*hildren need models rather than critics.

—*Joseph Joubert*

❧

*C*hildren's talent to endure stems from
their ignorance of alternatives.

—*Maya Angelou*

❧

*I*f children live with criticism, they learn to condemn.
If children live with hostility, they learn to fight.
If children live with fear, they learn to be apprehensive.
If children live with shame, they learn to feel guilty.
If children live with tolerance, they learn to be patient.
If children live with encouragement,
they learn to be confident.
If children live with praise, they learn to appreciate.
If children live with approval, they
learn to like themselves.
If children live with acceptance, they
learn to find love in the world.
If children live with sharing, they learn to be generous.

—*Dorothy L. Nolte*

*Y*ou cannot catch a child's spirit by running after it; you must stand still and for love it will soon itself return.

—*Arthur Miller*

🌀

*T*he whole art of teaching is only the art of awakening the natural curiosity of young minds for the purpose of satisfying it afterwards.

—*Anatole France*

🌀

*T*he illiterate of the 21st century will not be those who cannot read and write, but those who cannot learn, unlearn, and relearn.

—*Alvin Toffler*

🌀

*T*he secret of education is respecting the pupil.

—*Ralph Waldo Emerson*

🌀

*S*ome of us will give our children everything and nothing of ourselves.

—*Noah benShea*

*T*he object of education is to prepare the young
to educate themselves throughout their lives.

—*Robert Maynard Hutchins*

❧

*T*he rules of parents are all but three . . . Love, Limit,
and Let them be.

—*Elaine M. Ward*

❧

*T*o withhold demanding content from young children
between preschool and third grade has an effect which is
quite different from the one intended. It leaves advantaged
children with boring pabulum, and it condemns disadvan-
taged children to a permanent educational handicap
that grows worse over time.

—*Prof. E. D. Hirsch*

❧

*C*hildren need company and the company of themselves.
So do adults who want to keep the child in them alive.

—*Noah benShea*

❧

*E*ducation is a weapon, whose effect depends on
who holds it in his hands and at whom it is aimed.

—*Joseph Stalin*

*D*o not train youth to learn by harshness, but lead them to it by what amuses their minds. Then you may discover the peculiar bent of the genius of each.

—*Plato*

❧

*I*ntellectual growth should commence at birth and cease only at death.

—*Albert Einstein*

❧

*W*e teach what we like to learn and the reason many people go into teaching is vicariously to re-experience the primary joy experienced the first time they learned something they loved.

—*Stephen Brookfield*

❧

A mind is a fire to be kindled, not a vessel to be filled.

—*Plutarch*

❧

*W*e must teach our children to dream with their eyes open.

—*Harry Edwards*

*C*hildren are apt to live up to what you believe of them.

—*Lady Bird Johnson*

❈

*R*esearch shows that you begin learning in the womb and go right on learning until the moment you pass on. Your brain has a capacity for learning that is virtually limitless, which makes every human a potential genius.

—*Michael J. Gelb*

❈

*W*ithout education, you're not going anywhere in this world.

—*Malcolm X*

COLLABORATION
AND TEAMWORK

$\mathcal{N}$ow this is the law of the jungle—As old and true as the sky; And the wolf that keep it may prosper, But the wolf that shall break it must die. The strength of the pack is the wolf And the strength of the wolf is the pack.

—Rudyard Kipling

*W*e are all marching alone, together.

—*Noah benShea*

❧

*T*he nice thing about teamwork is that you always
have others on your side.

—*Margaret Carty*

❧

*T*eamwork is the fuel that allows common people
to attain uncommon results.

—*Unknown*

❧

*I*magine what a harmonious world it could be if every
single person, both young and old, shared a little
of what he is good at doing.

—*Quincy Jones*

❧

*D*ependent people need others to get what they want.
Independent people can get what they want through their
own efforts. Interdependent people combine their own
efforts with the efforts of others to achieve
their greatest success.

—*Stephen R. Covey*

❧

*Y*ou cannot succeed by yourself. It's hard
to find a rich hermit.

—*Jim Rohn*

*L*ight is the task where many share the toil.

—*Homer*

❦

*T*he secret is to work less as individuals and more as a
team. As a coach, I play not my eleven best,
but my best eleven.

—*Knute Rockne*

❦

A person who is filled with himself
cannot be increased by others.

—*Noah benShea*

❦

*P*eople rowing a boat don't have time to rock it.

—*Anonymous*

❦

*S*ticks in a bundle are unbreakable.

—*Kenyan proverb*

*Y*ou become successful by helping others
become successful.

—*Anonymous*

*T*he best team doesn't win nearly as often as the team
that gets along best.

—*Rob Gilbert*

❧

*A*lone we can do so little; together we can do so much.

—*Helen Keller*

❧

*T*eamwork is the fuel that allows common people
to attain uncommon results.

—*Andrew Carnegie*

❧

*W*e're inclined to think that others don't know
what we're just learning.

—*Noah benShea*

❧

*C*oming together is a beginning, staying together
is progress, and working together is success.

—*Henry Ford*

❧

*I*ndividuals play the game, but teams beat the odds.

—*US Navy SEALS*

*T*he way a team plays as a whole determines its success. You may have the greatest bunch of individual stars in the world, but if they don't play together, the club won't be worth a dime.

—*Babe Ruth*

🔹

*W*hen he took time to help the man up the mountain, lo, he scaled it himself.

—*Tibetan proverb*

🔹

*E*verybody on a championship team doesn't get publicity, but everyone can say he's a champion.

—*Earvin "Magic" Johnson*

🔹

*T*alent wins games, but teamwork and intelligence win championships.

—*Michael Jordan*

🔹

*M*ichael, if you can't pass, you can't play.

—*Coach Dean Smith to Michael Jordan in his freshman year at UNC*

🔹

*N*o one can whistle a symphony. It takes an orchestra to play it.

—*H. E. Luccock*

COMMUNICATION AND CONFLICT

*W*ords of love are
works of love.

—*William R. Alger*

*L*istening
is sometimes the most powerful thing
we can say to another.

—*Noah benShea*

⊠

*I*t is not how much we give but how much love
we put into giving.

—*Mother Teresa*

⊠

*Y*ou have to set the tone and the pace, define objectives
and strategies, demonstrate through personal example
what you expect from others.

—*Stanley C. Gault*

⊠

*Y*ou have it easily in your power to increase the sum
total of this world's happiness now. How? By giving a few
words of sincere appreciation to someone who is lonely or
discouraged. Perhaps you will forget tomorrow the kind
words you say today, but the recipient may
cherish them over a lifetime.

—*Dale Carnegie*

⊠

*G*entle words, quiet words, are after all the most
powerful words. They are more convincing,
more compelling, more prevailing.

—*W. Gladden*

*W*e offer others a chance to lighten their load
when we say little and listen loudly.

—*Noah benShea*

🔰

I don't care how great, how famous or successful a man
or woman may be, each hungers for applause.

—*George M. Adams*

🔰

*T*he word "no" carries a lot more meaning when spoken
by a parent who also knows how to say "yes."

—*Joyce Maynard*

🔰

*O*ur own burdens weigh less when we listen
to what is weighing on others.

—*Noah benShea*

🔰

*T*wo monologues do not make a dialogue.

—*Jeff Daly*

🔰

*N*o one would talk much in society if they knew
how often they misunderstood others.

—*Johann Wolfgang Von Goethe*

*T*he art of communication is the language of leadership.

—*James Humes*

◎

*T*here is no pleasure to me without communication:
It grieves me to have produced alone and
have no one to tell it to.

—*Michel Eyquem de Montaigne*

◎

*T*o effectively communicate, we must realize that we
are all different in the way we perceive the world
and use this understanding as a guide
to our communication with others.

—*Anthony Robbins*

◎

*H*aving manners isn't about being perfect
but perfecting ourselves.

—*Noah benShea*

◎

*N*othing is so simple that it cannot be misunderstood.

—*Jr. Teague*

$\mathcal{B}$e a good listener. Your ears will never
get you in trouble.

—*Frank Tyger*

$\mathcal{K}$eep away from people who try to belittle your
ambitions. Small people always do that, but the really
great make you feel that you, too, can become great.

—*Mark Twain*

$\mathcal{U}$se a sweet tongue, courtesy, and gentleness, and thou
mayest manage to guide an elephant with a hair.

—*Sa'di*

$\mathcal{L}$isten or thy tongue will keep thee deaf.

—*American Indian proverb*

$\mathcal{T}$he greatest compliment that was ever paid me
was when one asked me what I thought,
and attended to my answer.

—*Henry David Thoreau*

*T*he greatest gift you can give another is
the purity of your attention.

—*Richard Moss*

*C*ommunication does not begin with being understood,
but with understanding others.

—*W. Steven Brown*

⧗

*I*f speaking is silver, then listening is gold.

—*Turkish proverb*

⧗

*I*f you are looking for mercy, be merciful.
Be what you seek.

—*Noah benShea*

⧗

*L*istening is a magnetic and strange thing, a creative
force. The friends who listen to us are the ones we move
toward. When we are listened to, it creates us,
makes us unfold and expand.

—*Karl Menniger*

⧗

*W*e are the calm and the storm in our lives.

—*Noah benShea*

*W*hen you are listening to somebody, completely,
attentively, then you are listening not only
to the words, but also to the feeling of what
is being conveyed, to the whole of it, not part of it.

—*Jiddu Krishnamurti*

❦

*A*n essential part of true listening is the discipline
of bracketing, the temporary giving up or setting aside
of one's own prejudices, frames of reference and desires
so as to experience as far as possible the speaker's world
from the inside. Bracketing, a setting aside of the self,
also temporarily involves a total acceptance of the other.
Sensing this acceptance, the speaker will feel less and less
vulnerable and more and more inclined to open up
the inner recesses of his or her mind to the listener.
As this happens, speaker and listener begin to appreciate
each other more and more, and the duet dance
of love is begun again.

—*M. Scott Peck*

❦

*C*hildren have never been very good at listening to their
elders, but they have never failed to imitate them.

—*James Arthur Baldwin*

❦

*T*oo often we give children answers to remember
rather than problems to solve.

—*Roger Lewin*

*T*o know how to suggest is the art of teaching.

—*Henri-Frederic Amiel*

❧

*T*o give offense is to take offense.

—*Taoist teaching*

❧

*P*oliteness when we disagree is not agreement
any more than being rude is a convincing argument.

—*Noah benShea*

❧

*T*he seeds of the Argument Culture can be found
in our classrooms, where a teacher will introduce an article
or an idea . . . setting up debates where people learn not
to listen to each other because they're so busy
trying to win the debate.

—*Deborah Tannen*

❧

*T*he teacher who is indeed wise does not bid you
to enter the house of his wisdom but rather
leads you to the threshold of your mind.

—*Kahlil Gibran*

*T*he greatest good you can do for another is not just
to share your riches but to reveal to him his own.

—*Benjamin Disraeli*

❦

*E*ducation should be the process of helping everyone
to discover his uniqueness, to teach him how to develop
that uniqueness, and then to show him how to share it
because that's the only reason for having anything.

—*Leo Buscaglia*

❦

*T*he first duty of a lecturer: to hand you after an hour's
discourse a nugget of pure truth to wrap up between
the pages of your notebooks, and keep
on the mantlepiece forever.

—*Virginia Woolf*

❦

*T*he dream begins, most of the time, with a teacher
who believes in you, who tugs and pushes and leads you
on to the next plateau, sometimes poking you
with a sharp stick called truth.

—*Dan Rather*

❦

*W*e learn a great deal about life and its burdens
when we, by listening,
quietly help others to unpack theirs.

—*Noah benShea*

COMMUNITY

$\mathcal{T}$he best way to find
yourself is to lose yourself
in the service of others.

—*Mahatma Gandhi*

*W*e can be independent and still depend on others.

—*Noah benShea*

⚜

*O*ne's life has value so long as one attributes value
to the life of others.

—*Simone de Beauvoir*

⚜

*Y*ou cannot hope to build a better world
without improving the individuals.

—*Madam Marie Curie*

⚜

*E*veryone needs to be valued. Everyone has
the potential to give something back.

—*Diana, Princess of Wales*

⚜

*T*he moments we share with others
remind us that we are neighbors in time.

—*Noah benShea*

⚜

*T*he charity that is a trifle to us
can be precious to others.

—Homer

*I*n nothing do men more nearly approach the gods than
in doing good to their fellow men.

—*Marcus Tillius Cicero*

❧

*I*t is we who are lost
when we don't help others
to find their way.

—*Noah benShea*

❧

*G*ive what you have to somebody, it may be
better than you think.

—*Henry Wadsworth Longfellow*

❧

*T*he measure of a man is not in the number of his
servants, but in the number of people whom he serves.

—*Paul D. Moody*

❧

*B*ehold how good and how pleasant it is for brethren
to dwell together in unity.

—*Bible: Psalms 133:1*

❧

*W*e must, indeed, all hang together or, most assuredly,
we shall all hang separately.

—*Benjamin Franklin*

*W*e are not going to be able to operate our Spaceship
Earth successfully nor for much longer unless we see
it as a whole spaceship and our fate as common.
It has to be everybody or nobody.

—*R. Buckminster Fuller*

❧

*W*hen we offer others harbor, we calm our storms.
When we offer others a hand, we are lifted.

—*Noah benShea*

❧

*E*ither men will learn to live like brothers, or
they will die like beasts.

—*Max Lerner*

❧

*T*here is no such thing as a self-made man. You will
reach your goals only with the help of others.

—*George Shinn*

❧

*I*t is in the shelter of each other that the people live.

—*Irish proverb*

❧

*T*ell everyone what you want to do
and someone will want to help you do it.

—*W. Clement Stone*

The nice thing about teamwork is that you always
have others on your side.

—Margaret Carty

❧

Coming together is a beginning, staying together
is progress, and working together is success.

—Henry Ford

❧

The achievements of an organization are the results
of the combined effort of each individual.

—Vince Lombardi

❧

Don't agonize, organize.

—Florynce Kennedy

❧

Water, everywhere over the earth, flows to join
together. A single natural law controls it. Each human
is a member of a community and should work within it.

—I Ching (BC 1150)

❧

There is more than a verbal tie between the words
common, community, and communication.

—John Dewey

*T*he most important motive for work in school and in life is pleasure in work, pleasure in its result, and knowledge of the value of the result to the community.

—*Albert Einstein*

❦

A community is like a ship, everyone ought to be prepared to take the helm.

—*Henrik Ibsen*

❦

*I*n the end the aggressors always destroy themselves, making way for others who know how to cooperate and get along. Life is much less a competitive struggle for survival than a triumph of cooperation and creativity.

—*Fritjof Capra*

❦

*T*he role of the teacher remains the highest calling of a free people. To the teacher, America entrusts her most precious resource, her children.

—*Congresswoman Shirley Mount Hufstedler*

❦

*I*n a community, the total of the parts is greater than the sum.

—*Noah benShea*

COMPASSION

*C*ompassion is
the basis of morality.
—*Arthur Schopenhauer*

*T*he defining measure of the term "civilization" is how people with power treat people without power.

—*Noah benShea*

◼

I expect to pass through the world but once. Any good therefore that I can do, or any kindness I can show to any creature, let me do it now. Let me not defer it, for I shall not pass this way again.

—*Stephen Grellet*

◼

*K*indness is the highest wisdom.

—*The Talmud*

◼

*W*hat wisdom can you find that is greater than kindness?

—*Jean-Jacques Rousseau*

◼

*C*ompassion is when we cross the bridge from sympathy to empathy.

—*Noah benShea*

◼

*M*en are only as great as they are kind.

—*Elbert Hubbard*

𝒩o act of kindness, no matter how small,
is ever wasted.

—*Aesop*

❈

𝒪ur duty is to be useful, not according to our desires
but according to our powers.

—*Henri-Frederic Amiel*

❈

𝒯hinking of what to wear today?
Why not wear a warm heart and an open mind.

—*Noah benShea*

❈

𝒯here are two ways of spreading light: to be
the candle or the mirror that reflects it.

—*Edith Wharton*

❈

𝒲hat we have done for ourselves alone dies with us;
what we have done for others and the world
remains and is immortal.

—*Albert Pike*

$\mathcal{I}$t is the characteristic of the magnanimous man to ask no favor but to be ready to do kindness to others.

—*Aristotle*

❧

$\mathcal{T}$he best place to find a helping hand is at the end of your own arm.

—*Swedish proverb*

❧

$\mathcal{K}$indness is earned by helping someone who can never repay you.

—*Noah benShea*

❧

$\mathcal{C}$aring, that is, consideration for others, is a good life, a good society.

—*Confucius*

❧

$\mathcal{L}$ove—the more you share with others, the more you have.

—*Mother Teresa*

❧

$\mathcal{I}$t is one of the most beautiful compensations of this life that no person can sincerely try to help another without helping themselves.

—*Ralph Waldo Emerson*

*L*ove is God: that is the only truth
that I really recognize. Love equals God.

—*Mahatma Gandhi*

❈

*O*ur deeds determine us, as much as we
determine our deeds.

—*George Eliot*

❈

*L*ife is sorrow. Compassion the only path.

—*Buddha*

❈

*W*hen one reaches out to help another
he touches the face of God.

—*Walt Whitman*

❈

*P*rogress comes from caring more about what needs
to be done than about who gets the credit.

—*Dorothy Height*

❈

*K*indness in words creates confidence.
Kindness in thinking creates profoundness.
Kindness in giving creates love.

—*Lao Tzu*

There are lots of young men and women we would love
to have as students, the Nobel Prize winners, and it would
be a sin if society is deprived of the fruits of their work
down the road because those of us, today, who
could have helped, didn't.

—*Michael Bloomberg*

❋

There is a wonderful mythical law of nature
that the three things we crave most in life
—happiness, freedom, and peace of mind—
are always attained by giving
them to someone else.

—*Peyton Conway March*

❋

We are all members of one tribe,
the tribe of time and vulnerability.

—*Noah benShea*

❋

I don't know what your destiny will be,
but one thing I do know:
the only ones among you who will be really happy
are those who have sought and found how to serve.

—*Albert Schweitzer*

CRITICAL

$\mathcal{T}$he trouble with most of
us is that we would rather
be ruined by praise than
saved by criticism.

—Norman Vincent Peale

No one can make you feel inferior
without your consent.

—*Eleanor Roosevelt*

Opinions like to keep their own company.

—*Noah benShea*

It's kinda nice to be remembered by your peers and
your fans, because you can achieve a lot of success
and be a creep too! But we try to be nice . . . .

—*Karen Carpenter*

If we plant a flower or a shrub and water it daily it will
grow so tall that in time we shall need a spade and a hoe to
uproot it. It is just so, I think, when we commit a fault,
however small, each day, and do not cure ourselves of it.
It is true that we cannot be free from sin, but at least
let our sins not be always the same . . .

—*St. Teresa of Avila*

Their is no defense against criticism except obscurity.

—*Joseph Addison*

*C*riticism is an indispensable element of culture.
—*Theodor W. Adorno*

❧

*M*en will take almost any kind of criticism except
the observation that they have no sense of humor.
—*Steve Allen*

❧

*S*elf criticism must be my guide to action, and
the first rule for its employment is that in itself
it is not a virtue, only a procedure.
—*Kingsley Amis*

❧

*P*oetry is at bottom a criticism of life.
—*Matthew Arnold*

❧

*S*andwich every bit of criticism between
two layers of praise.
—*Mary Kay Ash*

❧

*T*here is less in this than meets the eye.
—*Tallulah Bankhead*

*T*o love without criticism is to be betrayed.

—*Djuna Barnes*

⚜

I have the "worst" ear for criticism; even when I have created a stage set I like, I "always" hear the woman in the back of the dress circle who says she doesn't like blue.

—*Cecil Beaton*

⚜

*N*o critic speaks as loudly or resonates more profoundly than our fears.

—*Noah benShea*

⚜

*T*he test of democracy is freedom of criticism.

—*David Ben-Gurion*

⚜

*F*ree yourself to hear criticism or enslave yourself to your fears.

—*Noah benShea*

⚜

I am perfectly happy to believe that nobody likes us but the public.

—*Rudolf Bing*

The rule in carving holds good as to criticism; never cut with a knife what you can cut with a spoon.

—*Charles Buxton*

❦

Don't take criticism to heart
but get to the heart of the criticism.

—*Noah benShea*

❦

If my books had been any worse I should not have been invited to Hollywood, and if they had been any better
I should not have come.

—*Raymond Chandler*

❦

Criticism is a misconception: we must read
not to understand others but to understand ourselves.

—*Emile M. Cioran*

❦

What we say about others is telling of us.

—*Noah benShea*

❦

Be kind and considerate with your criticism. . . . It's just as hard to write a bad book as it is to write a good book.

—*Malcolm Cowley*

*A*ll of us could take a lesson from the weather.
It pays no attention to criticism.

—*North DeKalb*

☒

*A*nimals are such agreeable friends—
they ask no questions, they pass no criticisms.

—*George Eliot*

☒

*C*riticism should not be querulous and wasting, all knife
and root-puller, but guiding, instructive, inspiring.

—*Ralph Waldo Emerson*

☒

*T*he World little knows how many thoughts and theories
which have passed through the mind of a scientific
investigator and have been crushed in silence
and secrecy of his own criticism.

—*Michael Faraday*

☒

*T*wo cheers for Democracy: one because it admits variety
and two because it permits criticism.

—*E. M. Forster*

*C*riticism is more effective when it sounds like praise.

—*Arnold Glasow*

🌾

*T*he devil is an optimist if he thinks
he can make people worse than they are.

—*Karl Kraus*

🌾

*C*riticism is more than cynicism given a voice.

—*Noah benShea*

🌾

*C*oughing in the theater is not a respiratory ailment.
It is a criticism.

—*Alan Jay Lerner*

🌾

*W*hat you said hurt me very much. I cried
all the way to the bank.

—*Liberace*

🌾

*C*ruelty is not necessarily good criticism
any more than kindness is necessarily praise.

—*Noah benShea*

I have never found, in a long experience of politics,
that criticism is ever inhibited by ignorance.

—*Harold Macmillan*

❦

*E*ducation is a crutch with which the foolish
attack the wise to prove that they are not idiots.

—*Karl Kraus*

❦

*I*n order to excel, you must also be prepared to work
hard and be willing to accept destructive criticism.
Without 100 percent dedication, you
won't be able to do this.

—*Willie Mays*

❦

*S*o who's perfect? . . . Washington had false teeth.
Franklin was nearsighted. Mussolini had syphilis.
Unpleasant things have been said about Walt Whitman
and Oscar Wilde. Tchaikovsky had his problems, too.
And Lincoln was constipated.

—*John O'Hara*

❦

*I*t is doubtless a vice to turn one's eye inward too much,
but I am my own comedy and tragedy.

—*Ralph Waldo Emerson*

*I*t is easy—terribly easy—to shake a man's faith
in himself. To take advantage of that, to break
a man's spirit is devil's work.

—*George Bernard Shaw*

❧

*W*hat other dungeon is so dark as one's own heart?
What jailer is so inexorable as oneself?

—*Nathanial Hawthorne*

❧

*S*elf love is an idolotry.

—*Elizabeth Hardwick*

❧

*N*o person loving or admiring himself is alone.

—*Theodor Reik*

❧

*E*very man supposes himself not to be
fully understood or appreciated.

—*Ralph Waldo Emerson*

❧

*L*ife, I fancy, would very often be insupportable
but for the luxury of self compassion.

—*George Jissing*

*I*t is not enough to understand what we ought to be,
unless we know what we are. And we don't understand
what we are unless we know what we ought to be.

—*T. S. Eliot*

⚘

*I*n life there is applause and attack.
These are tides of opinion, and like all tides,
are subject inevitably to ebb and flow.

—*Noah benShea*

⚘

*B*ut enough about me. Let's talk about you
and what you think of me.

—*Ed Koch*

⚘

*I*t is wisdom to know others. It is enlightenment
to know oneself.

—*Lao Tzu*

⚘

*K*now the enemy and know yourself and you can fight a
hundred battles with no dangers or defeat.

—*Sun Tzu*

*B*e what you are; this is the first step towards
becoming better than you are.

—*J.C. Hare*

❧

*I*ndividualization does not shut one out from the world,
but gathers the world to itself.

—*Carl Gustav Jung*

❧

*T*o avoid criticism, do nothing, say nothing, be nothing.

—*Elbert Hubbard*

❧

*T*hose whom we can love we can hate—
to others we are indifferent.

—*Henry David Thoreau*

❧

*T*o really know some one is to have loved
and hated him in turn.

—*Marcel Jouhandeau*

❧

*E*verything that frees our spirit without giving us
control of our selves is ruin-ness.

—*Johann Wolfgang Von Goethe*

Self deceit—is the refuge of the weak.

—*Louis de Caulaincourt*

❈

Part of me suspects I'm a loser, and the other part of me thinks I'm God Almighty.

—*John Lennon*

DISCIPLINE

$\mathcal{T}$he best discipline,
maybe the only discipline
that really works,
is self discipline.

—*Walter Kiechel III*

*D*iscipline in its highest notion is not punishment or
self-punishment. It is rather something seminal to the self.
It is our foundation. It is our architecture.
It give us structure. It allows us to steer
our energies and pull our wagon.

—*Noah benShea*

❈

*S*ome people regard discipline as a chore. For me, it is
a kind of order that sets me free to fly.

—*Julie Andrews*

❈

*D*iscipline must come through liberty. We do not
consider an individual disciplined only when he has
been rendered as artificially silent as a mute and
as immovable as a paralytic. He is an individual
annihilated, not disciplined.

—*Maria Montessori*

❈

*G*ood discipline is more than just punishing
or laying down the law. It is liking
children and letting them see that they
are liked. It is caring enough about them
to provide good, clear rules
for their protection.

—*Stanley I. Greenspan*

The best time to punish
is not when we're at our maddest,
but that's usually when we do it.

—Nancy Samalin

❧

Age acquires no value save through
thought and discipline.

—James Truslow Adams

❧

A mode of conduct, a standard of courage, discipline,
fortitude and integrity can do a great deal
to make a woman beautiful.

—Jacqueline Bisset

❧

Endurance is one of the most difficult disciplines,
but it is to the one who endures
that the final victory comes.

—Buddha

❧

It is not crazy to think of discipline as a chariot.
Without discipline we would drive ourselves crazy.

—Noah benShea

*T*he discipline of the writer is to learn to be still
and listen to what his subject has to tell him.

—*Rachel Carson*

▓

*I*t takes great discipline to slowly peel a moment.
An eternity is any moment opened with patience.

—*Noah benShea*

▓

*E*rror is discipline through which we advance.

—*William Ellery Channing*

▓

*E*rror is a discipline in the science of inquiry.

—*Noah benShea*

▓

*D*iscipline is a symbol of caring to a child. Discipline is
guidance. If there is love, there is no such thing
as being too tough with a child.

—*Bette Davis*

▓

*S*uccess isn't measured by money or power or social rank.
Success is measured by your discipline and inner peace.

—*Mike Ditka*

*A*s we grow older, we must discipline ourselves to
continue expanding, broadening, learning,
keeping our minds active and open.

—*Clint Eastwood*

❈

*D*iscipline, to ourselves or others,
is not loving to be tough
but tough love.

—*Noah benShea*

❈

*T*he great end of education is to discipline rather than to
furnish the mind; to train it to the use of its own powers,
rather than fill it with the accumulation of others.

—*Tryon Edwards*

❈

*G*enius at first is little more than a great
capacity for receiving discipline.

—*George Eliot*

❈

*N*o steam or gas ever drives anything until it is
confined. No Niagara is ever turned into light
and power until it is tunneled. No life ever grows
until it is focused, dedicated, disciplined.

—*Harry Emerson Fosdick*

*N*o restraint. No release.

—*Noah benShea*

⚘

*W*ithout discipline, there's no life at all.

—*Katharine Hepburn*

⚘

*S*eek freedom and become captive of your desires. Seek discipline and find your liberty.

—*Frank Herbert*

⚘

*T*he discipline of writing something down is the first step toward making it happen.

—*Lee Iacocca*

⚘

*D*iscipline and concentration are a matter of being interested.

—*Tom Kite*

⚘

*M*anagers must have the discipline not to keep pulling up the flowers to see if their roots are healthy.

—*Robert Townsend*

*D*iscipline is the soul of an army.
It makes small numbers formidable,
procures success to the weak
and esteem to all.

—*George Washington*

🌂

*C*heerfulness in most cheerful people is the rich
and satisfying result of strenuous discipline.

—*Edwin Percy Whipple*

🌂

*W*ith self-discipline most anything is possible.

—*Theodore Roosevelt*

DIVERSITY, CULTURE, AND LANGUAGE

*W*hat we have to do
is to find a way
to celebrate our diversity
and debate our differences
without fracturing our
communities.

—*Hillary Rodham Clinton*

*U*nderstanding is living in a house
where every room has a point of view.

—*Noah benShea*

❈

*I*n crucial things—unity,
in important things—diversity,
in all things—generosity.

—*George H. W. Bush*

❈

*T*he diversity of the phenomena of nature is so great, and
the treasures hidden in the heavens so rich, precisely
in order that the human mind shall never be
lacking in fresh nourishment.

—*Johannes Kepler*

❈

*C*ircumstances.

—*Stephen Bayley*

❈

*C*ulture is not a biologically transmitted complex. If we
justify war, it is because all people always justify the traits
of which they find themselves possessed, not because war
will bear an objective examination of its merits.

—*Ruth Benedict*

A giant is anyone able to see past their own opinion.
—*Noah benShea*

❈

*N*o culture can live if it attempts to be exclusive.
—*Mahatma Gandhi*

❈

*W*hoever controls the media—the images—
controls the culture.
—*Allen Ginsberg*

❈

A culture is not an abstract thing.
It is a living, evolving process.
—*Mary Robinson*

❈

*T*he Law of Raspberry Jam:
The wider any culture is spread,
the thinner it gets.
—*Alvin Toffler*

❈

*W*e all have different beliefs.
All belief has believing in common.
—*Noah benShea*

*L*anguage is a city to the building of which
every human being brought a stone.

—*Ralph Waldo Emerson*

❧

*I*t is not how many languages you can speak
but whether you have anything to say.

—*Noah benShea*

❧

*Y*ou are as many a person as languages you know.

—*Armenian proverb*

❧

*T*he finest command of language
is often shown by saying nothing.

—*Roger W. Babson*

❧

*L*anguage is a skin: It is as if I had words instead
of fingers, or fingers at the tip of my words.
My language trembles with desire.

—*Roland Barthes*

❧

*A*cting is not my language at all.

—*Mikhail Baryshnikov*

*W*ords are often like buoys.
They tell others where we are
but little of what lies below.

—*Noah benShea*

❈

*D*rawing on my fine command of language,
I said nothing.

—*Robert Benchley*

❈

*I*NTERPRETER, *n.* One who enables two persons
of different languages to understand each other
by repeating to each what it would have been
to the interpreter's advantage for
the other to have said.

—*Ambrose Bierce*

❈

A language . . . is a more ancient and
inevitable thing than any state.

—*Joseph Brodsky*

❈

*L*anguage is the road map of a culture. It tells you where
its people come from and where they are going.

—*Rita Mae Brown*

*T*he unconscious is the ocean of the unsayable,
of what has been expelled from the land of language,
removed as a result of ancient prohibitions.

—*Italo Calvino*

⬧

*L*anguage is a process of free creation; its laws and
principles are fixed, but the manner in which the
principles of generation are used is free and infinitely
varied. Even the interpretation and use of
words involves a process of free creation.

—*Noam Chomsky*

⬧

*T*he liberation of language is rooted
in the liberation of ourselves.

—*Mary Daly*

⬧

*L*anguage is not only the vehicle of thought,
it is a great and efficient instrument in thinking.

—*Sir Humphrey Davy*

⬧

*W*hen one man dies,
one chapter is not torn out of the book,
but translated into a better language.

—*John Donne*

*T*here is a fear
—common to all English-only speakers—
that the chief purpose of foreign languages
is to make fun of us.

—*Barbara Ehrenreich*

❧

*L*anguage is the archives of history.

—*Ralph Waldo Emerson*

❧

*E*ngland and America are two countries
separated by the same language.

—*George Bernard Shaw*

13

GIFTED AND TALENTED

---

*T*alent is God-given.
Be humble.
Fame is man-given.
Be grateful.
Conceit is self-given.
Be careful.

—*John Wooden*

*B*ecause life is a gift, all of us are gifted.

—*Noah benShea*

⚜

*I*t takes little talent to see clearly what lies under one's nose, a good deal of it to know in which direction to point that organ.

—*W. H. Auden*

⚜

*M*ediocrity knows nothing higher than itself, but talent instantly recognizes genius.

—*Sir Arthur Conan Doyle*

⚜

*E*very man has his own vocation; talent is the call.

—*Ralph Waldo Emerson*

⚜

*W*e are told that talent creates its own opportunities. But it sometimes seems that intense desire creates not only its own opportunities, but its own talents.

—*Eric Hoffer*

⚜

*W*isdom is where we have the wisdom to find it.

—*Noah benShea*

*E*veryone has talent. What is rare is the courage
to follow the talent to the dark place where it leads.

—*Erica Jong*

❧

*E*veryone according to their talent
and every talent according to its work.

—*French proverb*

❧

I thought my talent would transcend
my outspokenness. I was wrong.

—*Mickey Rourke*

❧

*N*o matter how gifted we are
none of us are a gift to others
if we're wrapped up in ourselves.

—*Noah benShea*

❧

*G*reat talents are the most lovely and often the most
dangerous fruits on the tree of humanity.
They hang upon the most slender twigs
that are easily snapped off.

—*Carl Gustav Jung*

*U*se what talent you possess:
the woods would be very silent
if no birds sang except those that sang best.

—*Henry Van Dyke*

*A*nything we can learn is a gift
considering the cost of ignorance.

—*Noah benShea*

*A*ttitude is more important than the past, than
education, than money, than circumstances,
than what people do or say. It is more important
than appearance, giftedness, or skill.

—*Charles Swindoll*

*P*eople with great gifts are easy to find,
but symmetrical and balanced ones never.

—*Ralph Waldo Emerson*

*T*here is rarely a creative man who does not have to pay
a high price for the divine spark of his great gifts . . . the
human element is frequently bled for the benefit
of the creative element.

—*Carl Gustav Jung*

*Y*ou better like your gifts
because you're going to pay for them.

—*Noah benShea*

❈

*T*he world is put back by the death of every
one who has to sacrifice the development
of his or her peculiar gifts to conventionality.

—*Florence Nightingale*

❈

*T*he barriers are not erected which can say
to aspiring talents and industry, "Thus far and no farther."

—*Ludwig van Beethoven*

❈

*T*o be wise we only have to go in search of our ignorance.

—*Noah benShea*

❈

*P*eople who are unable to motivate themselves must be
content with mediocrity, no matter how
impressive their other talents.

—*Andrew Carnegie*

❈

*T*he good teacher discovers the natural gifts of his pupils
and liberates them. The true leader makes his followers
twice the men they were before.

—*Stephen Neil*

*B*eyond talent lie all the usual words: discipline, love,
luck—but, most of all, endurance.

—*James Arthur Baldwin*

⚘

*T*he toughest thing about success is that you've
got to keep on being a success.

—*Irving Berlin*

⚘

A great deal of talent is lost to the world
for the want of a little courage.

—*Sydney Smith*

⚘

*H*ide not your talents, they for use were made.
What's a sundial in the shade?

—*Benjamin Franklin*

⚘

*B*lessed are they who have the gift of making friends,
for it is one of God's best gifts. It involves many things,
but above all, the power of going out of one's self,
and appreciating whatever is noble
and loving in another.

—*Thomas Hughes*

⚘

*T*hings don't have to be good for us to be great.

—*Noah benShea*

*W*hen I examine myself and my methods of thought,
I come to the conclusion that the gift of fantasy
has meant more to me than any talent
for abstract, positive thinking.

—*Albert Einstein*

❦

*W*hat you are is God's gift to you,
what you do with yourself
is your gift to God.

—*Anonymous*

GOSSIP

14

𝒩o one tries to steal
your troubles and no one
can take your good deeds.
—*Yiddish folk saying*

*G*ossip is poison given orally.

—*Noah benShea*

§

*I*t takes your enemy and your friend, working together,
to hurt you to the heart; the one to slander you and
the other to get the news to you.

—*Mark Twain*

§

*T*here is so much good in the worst of us, and so much
bad in the best of us, that it ill behooves any
of us to find fault with the rest of us.

—*James Truslow Adams*

§

A gossip is one who talks to you about others; a bore is
one who talks to you about himself; and a brilliant
conversationalist is one who talks
to you about yourself.

—*Lisa Kirk*

§

*O*ne eyewitness is better than ten hearsayers.

—*Titus Maccius Plautus*

*A*nd all who told it added something new, and all who
heard it, made enlargements too.

—*Alexander Pope*

❧

*W*hoever gossips to you will gossip about you.

—*Spanish proverb*

❧

*C*ount not him among your friends who will
retell your privacies to the world.

—*Pubilius Syrus*

❧

*W*hat you keep by you, you may change and mend
but words, once spoken, can never be recalled.

—*Earl of Roscommon*

❧

*L*ive in such a way that you would not be ashamed
to sell your parrot to the town gossip.

—*Will Rogers*

❧

*T*he words you speak today should be soft and tender . . .
for tomorrow you may have to eat them.

—*Unknown*

If you haven't got anything nice to say about anybody,
come sit next to me.

—*Alice Roosevelt Longworth*

✻

What you don't see with your eyes,
don't witness with your mouth.

—*Yiddish proverb*

✻

What is told in the ear of a man is often heard
100 miles away.

—*Chinese proverb*

✻

No one gossips about other people's secret virtues.

—*Bertrand Russell*

✻

If you reveal your secrets to the wind, you should not
blame the wind for revealing them to the trees.

—*Kahlil Gibran*

✻

If you add to the truth, you subtract from it.

—*The Talmud*

The easiest way to keep a secret is without help.
—*Unknown*

❦

The moments we share with others
remind us we are neighbors in time.
—*Noah benShea*

❦

Gossip needn't be false to be evil—there's a lot of truth
that shouldn't be passed around.
—*Frank A. Clark*

❦

Trying to squash a rumor is like trying to unring a bell.
—*Shana Alexander*

❦

Whether it's boot camp or ballet camp,
we all share the same emotional wardrobe.
—*Noah benShea*

❦

A rumor without a leg to stand on
will get around some other way.
—*John Tudor*

*T*hree may keep a secret if two are dead.

—*Benjamin Franklin*

❧

*T*here are a terrible lot of lies going about the world, and the worst of it is that half of them are true.

—*Sir Winston Churchill*

❧

*T*he biggest liar in the world is They Say.

—*Douglas Malloch*

LEADERSHIP

$\mathcal{Y}$ou do not lead by
hitting people over the
head—that's assault;
not leadership.

—*Dwight D. Eisenhower*

𝒜ll leadership begins with self-leadership.

—*Noah benShea*

❧

𝓔ducation is the mother of leadership.

—*Wendell L. Willkie*

❧

𝓛eadership is getting someone to do what they don't want to do, to achieve what they want to achieve.

—*Tom Landry*

❧

𝒩ever let your sense of morals get in the way of doing what's right.

—*Isaac Asimov*

❧

𝓛eadership and learning are indispensable to each other.

—*John F. Kennedy*

❧

𝓜en make history, and not the other way around. In periods where there is no leadership, society stands still. Progress occurs when courageous, skillful leaders seize the opportunity to change things for the better.

—*Harry S Truman*

*L*eadership has a harder job to do than just choose sides.
It must bring sides together.

—*Jesse Jackson*

❧

I start with the premise that the function of leadership
is to produce more leaders, not more followers.

—*Ralph Nader*

❧

*W*hether a man is burdened by power or enjoys power;
whether he is trapped by responsibility or made free by it;
whether he is moved by other people and outer forces or
moves them—this is of the essence of leadership.

—*Theodore H. White*

❧

A leader doesn't rule over but lifts up.

—*Noah benShea*

❧

*G*ood leadership consists in showing average people how
to do the work of superior people.

—*John D. Rockefeller*

*N*early all men can stand adversity, but if you want to test a man's character, give him power.

—*Abraham Lincoln*

❧

*C*haracter cannot be developed in ease and quiet. Only through experience of trial and suffering can the soul be strengthened, ambition inspired, and success achieved.

—*Helen Keller*

❧

*G*ood leaders make people feel that they're at the very heart of things, not at the periphery.

—*Warren Bennis*

❧

*T*he very essence of leadership is that you have to have a vision.

—*Theodore Hesburgh*

❧

*T*he great leaders are like the best conductors— they reach beyond the notes to reach the magic in the players.

—*Blaine Lee*

The ultimate leader is one who is willing to develop
people to the point that they eventually surpass
him or her in knowledge and ability.
—Fred A. Manske, Jr.

❧

Leadership is a combination of strategy and character.
If you must be without one, be without the strategy.
—General H. Norman Schwarzkopf

❧

Skill in the art of communication is crucial
to a leader's success. He can accomplish nothing
unless he can communicate effectively.
—Norman Allen

❧

The first task of a leader is to keep hope alive.
—Joe Batten

❧

When firmness is sufficient, rashness is unnecessary.
—Napoleon Bonaparte

❧

Pull the string, and it will follow wherever you wish.
Push it, and it will go nowhere at all.
—Dwight D. Eisenhower

*T*he highest of distinctions is service to others.

—*King George VI*

❧

A leader is one who knows the way, goes the way
and shows the way.

—*John C. Maxwell*

❧

*T*hose that rule must hear and be deaf,
must see and be blind.

—*German proverb*

❧

*T*he challenge of leadership is to be strong, but not rude;
be kind, but not weak; be bold, but not bully; be
thoughtful, but not lazy; be humble, but not timid;
be proud, but not arrogant; have humor,
but without folly.

—*Jim Rohn*

❧

*O*utstanding leaders appeal to the hearts of their
followers—not their minds.

—*Unknown*

*T*he mediocre teacher tells.
The good teacher explains.
The superior teacher demonstrates.
The great teacher inspires.

—*William Arthur Ward*

🌜

*I*f you want to move people, it has to be toward a vision
that's positive for them, that taps important values,
that gets them something they desire, and it has
to be presented in a compelling way that
they feel inspired to follow.

—*Martin Luther King, Jr.*

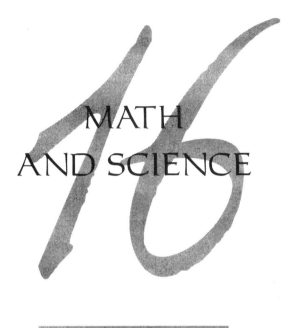

MATH AND SCIENCE

$\mathcal{T}$he essence of
mathematics
is not to make simple
things complicated,
but to make complicated
things simple.

—*S. Gudder*

*S*cience is formalized inquiry and a reminder that in life there are good answers but great questions.

—*Noah benShea*

❈

*M*athematics is the gate and key to the sciences.

—*Roger Bacon*

❈

*M*athematics is the handwriting on the human consciousness of the very Spirit of Life itself.

—*Claude Bragdon*

❈

*T*he essence of mathematics resides in its freedom.

—Georg Cantor

❈

*N*umbers are the free creation of the human mind.

—*Richard Dedekind*

❈

*P*ure mathematics is, in its way, the poetry of logical ideas.

—*Albert Einstein*

*P*eople who don't count won't count.

—*Anatole France*

❧

*T*he Universe is a grand book which cannot be read until one first learns to comprehend the language and become familiar with the characters in which it is composed. It is written in the language of mathematics.

—*Galileo*

❧

A mathematician, like a painter or a poet, is a maker of patterns. If his patterns are more permanent than theirs, it is because they are made with ideas.

—*G. H. Hardy*

❧

*I*n most sciences one generation tears down what another has built and what one has established another undoes. In mathematics alone each generation adds a new story to the old structure.

—*Herman Henkel*

❧

*W*hen you can measure what you are talking about and express it in numbers, you know something about it.

—*Lord Kelvin*

$\mathcal{M}$athematics has been most advanced by those who
distinguished themselves by intuition rather
than by rigorous proofs.

—*Felix Klein*

▨

$\mathcal{I}$n a time when much of the world's geography has been
explored, and space exploration is restricted
to astronauts, mathematics offers fertile
ground for exploring the unknown.

—*Walter Meyer*

▨

$\mathcal{T}$he moving power of mathematical invention is not
reasoning but imagination.

—*Augustus de Morgan*

▨

$\mathcal{I}$ do not know what I may appear to the world, but
to myself I seem to have been only a boy playing
on the seashore, and diverting myself now and
then finding a smoother pebble or a prettier sea
shell than ordinary whilst the great ocean
of truth lay all undiscovered before me.

—*Isaac Newton*

J love mathematics . . . principally because it is
beautiful, because man has breathed his spirit
of play into it, and because it has given him
his greatest game the encompassing
of the infinite.

—*Rozco Peter*

❈

*N*umbers are the highest degree of knowledge.
It is knowledge itself.

—*Plato*

❈

A mathematician who is not also something of a poet
will never be a complete mathematician.

—*Karl Weierstrass*

❈

*A*ll our science, measured against reality,
is primitive and childlike—and yet
it is the most precious thing we have.

—*Albert Einstein*

❈

*A*s soon as questions of will or decision or reason or
choice or action arise, human science is at a loss.

—*Noam Chomsky*

*T*he most beautiful thing we can experience is the mysterious. It is the source of all true art and science.

—*Albert Einstein*

❧

*I*n science the credit goes to the man who convinces the world, not the man to whom the idea first occurs.

—*Sir Francis Darwin*

❧

*G*ive me a lever long enough and a fulcrum on which to place it, and I shall move the world.

—*Archimedes*

❧

*E*very inquiry must question the blindness of its perspective. Archimedes had an idea that could move the world but had nowhere to stand.

—*Noah benShea*

❧

*T*here is a single light of science, and to brighten it anywhere is to brighten it everywhere.

—*Isaac Asimov*

❧

*E*very great advance in science has issued from a new audacity of imagination.

—*John Dewey*

PERSONAL AND PROFESSIONAL DEVELOPMENT

*W*e can't become what we need to be by remaining what we are.
—*Oprah Winfrey*

*N*o one ever got to be a better teacher
who wasn't working on being a better person.

—*Noah benShea*

§

*T*o laugh often and much
To win the respect of intelligent people
and the affection of children
To earn the appreciation of honest critics
and endure the betrayal of false friends
To appreciate beauty, to find the best in others
To leave the world a bit better, whether by
a healthy child, a garden patch, or
a redeemed social condition
To know that even one life has breathed easier
because you have lived
This is to have succeeded.

—*Ralph Waldo Emerson*

§

I find that the harder I work, the more luck
I seem to have.

—*Thomas Jefferson*

§

*D*o what you can, with what you have, where you are.

—*Theodore Roosevelt*

A pessimist sees the difficulty in every opportunity; an optimist sees the opportunity in every difficulty.

—*Sir Winston Churchill*

❈

*W*hen you are aspiring to the highest place, it is honorable to reach the second or even the third rank.

—*Marcus Tullius Cicero*

❈

*T*hey can conquer who believe they can.

—*Virgil*

❈

*O*nly those who risk going too far can possibly find out how far one can go.

—*T. S. Eliot*

❈

*T*hat best portion of a man's life: his little, nameless, unremembered acts of kindness and love.

—*William Wordsworth*

❈

*Y*ou gain strength, experience, and confidence by every experience where you really stop to look fear in the face . . . . You must do the thing you cannot do.

—*Eleanor Roosevelt*

*I*t's the action, not the fruit of the action, that's important. You have to do the right thing. It may not be in your power, may not be in your time, that there'll be any fruit. But that doesn't mean you stop doing the right thing. You may never know what results come from your action. But if you do nothing, there will be no result.

— *Mahatma Gandhi*

☙

*T*he marvelous richness of human experience would lose something of rewarding joy if there were no limitations to overcome. The hilltop hour would not be half so wonderful if there were no dark valleys to traverse.

—*Helen Keller*

☙

*E*verybody can be great . . . because anybody can serve. You don't have to have a college degree to serve. You don't have to make your subject and verb agree to serve. You only need a heart full of grace. A soul generated by love.

—*Martin Luther King, Jr.*

☙

*O*nly fears and mushrooms grow when they are fed darkness.

—*Noah benShea*

*O*bstacles are those frightful things you see
when you take your eyes off your goal.

—*Henry Ford*

❈

*A*lways continue the climb. It is possible for you to do
whatever you want if you first get to know who you are
and are willing to work with a power that is greater
than ourselves to do it.

—*Oprah Winfrey*

❈

*F*or all sad words of tongue and pen, the saddest are
those "It might have been."

—*John Greenleaf Whittier*

❈

*A*nd in the end it's not the years in your life that count.
It's the life in your years.

—*Abraham Lincoln*

❈

*Y*ou must be the change you wish to see in the world.

—*Mahatma Gandhi*

*S*ome of us grow so comfortable with our blindness
that the thought of seeing scares us.

—*Noah benShea*

☒

*W*hat counts is not necessarily the size of the dog in the
fight—it's the size of the fight in the dog.

—*Dwight D. Eisenhower*

☒

*Y*ou see things and say, "Why?", but I dream things
and say, "Why not?"

—*George Bernard Shaw*

☒

*I*t is not what they take away from you that counts.
It's what you do with what you have left.

—*Hubert Humphrey*

☒

*A*ll you need in life is ignorance and confidence,
and then success is sure.

—*Mark Twain*

☒

*M*y own experience and development deepen every day
my conviction that our moral progress may be measured
by the degree in which we sympathize with individual
suffering and individual joy.

—*George Eliot*

$\mathcal{T}$he antidote to hubris, to overweening pride, is irony,
that capacity to discover and systematize ideas. Or, as
Emerson insisted, the development of consciousness,
consciousness, consciousness.

—*Ralph Ellison*

❧

$\mathcal{W}$e are born deep. Some of us grow shallow.

—*Noah benShea*

❧

$\mathcal{T}$he human face is the organic seat of beauty. . . .
It is the register of value in development,
a record of Experience . . .

—*Eliza Wood Burhans Farnham*

❧

$\mathcal{T}$o me, the function and duty of a quality human being is
the sincere and honest development of one's potential.

—*Bruce Lee*

❧

$\mathcal{I}$'ve always believed in the adage that the secret
of eternal youth is arrested development.

—*Alice Roosevelt Longworth*

*B*y virtue of being born to humanity, every human being
has a right to the development and fulfillment
of his potentialities as a human being.

—*Ashley Montagu*

⚜

*I*f education is always to be conceived along the same
antiquated lines of a mere transmission of knowledge,
there is little to be hoped from it. . . . For what is the
use of transmitting knowledge if the individual's
total development lags behind?

—*Maria Montessori*

⚜

*T*here are very few human beings who receive the truth,
complete and staggering, by instant illumination. Most of
them acquire it fragment by fragment, on a small scale,
by successive developments, cellularly,
like a laborious mosaic.

—*Anaïs Nin*

⚜

*O*nly surround yourself with people who
will lift you higher.

—*Oprah Winfrey*

⚜

*I*f two people discover each other's blindness,
it is already growing light.

—*Noah benShea*

READING AND WRITING

A bookstore is one of the
only pieces of evidence we
have that people are
still thinking.

—*Jerry Seinfeld*

*A*ny moment spent reading to a child before bed
is a joy forever young.

—*Noah benShea*

☒

*T*he man who does not read good books has no
advantage over the man who cannot read them.

—*Mark Twain*

☒

*J*ournal writing is a voyage to the interior.

—*Christina Baldwin*

☒

*H*ow many a man has dated a new era in his life
from the reading of a book.

—*Henry David Thoreau*

☒

*I*f you would not be forgotten,
as soon as you are rotten,
either write things worth reading
or do things worth the writing.

—*Benjamin Franklin*

☒

*R*eading furnishes the mind only with materials of
knowledge; it is thinking that makes what we read ours.

—*John Locke*

*C*hildren without words are licked before they start. They are the legion of the young wordless in urban and rural slums. Most of them have never heard words used in other than rudimentary ways related to physical needs and functions. Children deprived of words become dropouts deprived of hope who often behave delinquently. Amateur censors blame delinquency on reading immoral books and magazines, when in fact, the inability to read anything is the basic trouble.

—*Peter S. Jennison*

❈

*T*he pen is the tongue of the mind.

—*Miguel de Cervantes*

❈

*Y*ou don't write because you want to say something; you write because you've got something to say.

—*F. Scott Fitzgerald*

❈

I suggest that the only books that influence us are those for which we are ready, and which have gone a little further down our particular path than we have gone ourselves.

—*E. M. Forster*

*W*ear the old coat and buy the new book.

—*Austin Phelps*

⚜

*S*ome books are to be tasted, others to be swallowed,
and some few to be chewed and digested.

—*Francis Bacon*

⚜

*T*he decline of literature indicates
the decline of a nation.

—*Johann Wolfgang Von Goethe*

⚜

A book is a mirror: if an ape looks into it
an apostle is hardly likely to look out.

—*G. C. Lichtenberg*

⚜

*S*ome of us read too much into things
but never read the writing on the wall.

—*Noah benShea*

⚜

*F*or books are more than books, they are the life
The very heart and core of ages past,
The reason why men lived and worked and died,
The essence and quintessence of their lives.

—*Amy Lowell*

*A*ll good books are alike in that they are truer than if
they had really happened and after you are finished
reading one you will feel that all that happened to you
and afterwards it all belongs to you; the good and the bad,
the ecstasy, the remorse, and sorrow, the people and
the places and how the weather was.

—*Ernest Hemingway*

❦

I always begin at the left with the opening word
of the sentence and read toward the right
and I recommend this method.

—*James Thurber*

❦

*W*hen the Day of Judgment dawns and the great
conquerors and lawyers and statesmen come to receive
their rewards—their crowns, their laurels, their names
carved indelibly upon imperishable marble—
the Almighty will turn to Peter and will say,
not without a certain envy when he sees us
coming with our books under our arms,
"Look, these need no reward. We have nothing
to give them here. They have loved reading."

—*Virginia Woolf*

*R*ead not to contradict and confute; nor to believe and take for granted; nor to find talk and discourse; but to weigh and consider.

—*Francis Bacon*

⊠

*M*any people read, but it is the wise who can read themselves.

—*Noah benShea*

RESPONSIBILITY

*T*he willingness to accept
responsibility for one's
own life is the source from
which self-respect springs.

—*Joan Didion*

*C*aring and not caring are contagious.

—*Noah benShea*

❧

I am responsible. Although I may not be able to prevent the worst from happening, I am responsible for my attitude toward the inevitable misfortunes that darken life. Bad things do happen; how I respond to them defines my character and the quality of my life. I can choose to sit in perpetual sadness, immobilized by the gravity of my loss, or I can choose to rise from the pain and treasure the most precious gift I have—life itself.

—*Walter Anderson*

❧

*I*f you take responsibility for yourself you will develop a hunger to accomplish your dreams.

—*Les Brown*

❧

*R*esponsibility walks hand in hand with capacity and power.

—*Josiah Gilbert Holland*

❧

I believe that every right implies a responsibility; every opportunity an obligation; every possession, a duty.

—*John D. Rockefeller*

*Y*ou cannot change the circumstances, the seasons,
  or the wind, but you can change yourself.
  That is something you have charge of.

—*Jim Rohn*

❈

*M*an is condemned to be free; because once thrown
into the world, he is responsible for everything he does.

—*Jean-Paul Sartre*

❈

*M*an must cease attributing his problems to his
environment, and learn again to exercise his will—
  his personal responsibility.

—*Albert Schweitzer*

❈

*I*f you don't invest very much, then defeat doesn't hurt
  very much and winning is not very exciting.

—*Dick Vermeil*

❈

*T*here is only one way to succeed in anything and
  that is to give everything.

—*Vince Lombardi*

*E*ach profession has its responsibilities as well as its privileges. One who gains confidence of others also assumes responsibilities toward them.

—*Alexis Lawrence Romanoff*

❧

*W*e are responsible for actions performed in response to circumstances for which we are not responsible.

—*Allan Massie*

❧

*M*ost of us are the load we are carrying.

—*Noah benShea*

❧

A teacher affects eternity; he can never tell where his influence stops.

—*Henry B. Adams*

❧

*L*ife is amazing: and the teacher had better prepare himself to be a medium for that amazement.

—*Edward Blishen*

❧

*W*hat office is there which involves more responsibility, which requires more qualifications, and which ought, therefore, to be more honourable, than that of teaching?

—*Harriet Martineau*

*S*uccess on any major scale requires you to accept
responsibility . . . in the final analysis, the one quality
that all successful people have . . . is the ability
to take on responsibility.

—*Michael Korda*

❦

*Y*ou cannot escape the responsibility of tomorrow
by evading it today.

—*Abraham Lincoln*

❦

*T*he reward of one duty is the power to fulfill another.

—*George Eliot*

❦

*W*here there are no rights, there are no duties.

—*Henri-Benjamin Constant de Rebecque*

❦

*T*oo many of us care more about being right
than doing right.

—*Noah benShea*

❦

I am only one; but still I am one. I cannot do
everything, but still I can do something;
I will not refuse to do something I can do.

—*Helen Keller*

SCHOOL SAFETY

Security is mostly
superstition.

—*Helen Keller*

*A*nger locks us in our house
and then burns down the house.

—*Noah benShea*

⚥

*H*ope comes when teachers decide to do something
about safer schools. Hope comes when everybody at school
works for a more secure environment. Hope comes when
you stop wishing and decide to work toward a more
security-conscious vision of the future.
Focus not on the way things are
but on the way you wish things to be.

—*Chester L. Quarles*

⚥

*E*veryone believes very easily whatever
they fear or desire.

—*Jean de La Fontaine*

⚥

*K*eep your fears to yourself,
but share your courage with others.

—*Robert Louis Stevenson*

⚥

*W*ho can hope to be safe? Who sufficiently cautious?
Guard himself as he may, every moment's an ambush.

—*Horace*

$\mathcal{H}$e is safe from danger who is on guard even when safe.
—*Publilius Syrus*

❦

$\mathcal{I}$ would give all my fame for a pot of ale and safety.
—*Shakespeare*

❦

$\mathcal{A}$ ship in harbor is safe, but that is not
what ships are built for.
—*John A. Shedd*

❦

$\mathcal{N}$ine-tenths of mankind are more afraid of
violence than anything else.
—*Walter Bagehot*

❦

$\mathcal{V}$iolence is lowest in schools with effective discipline
systems that mete out punishment swiftly
and consistently . . .
—*Kathy Koch*

❦

$\mathcal{W}$hen we see violent imagery over and over, it works
the same way as a Toyota commercial. It sells that image.
—*Paul Klite*

*E*very American has seen hundreds of films, hundreds of
depictions, thousands of cartoons. Millions
don't go out and shoot people.

—*Steve Brenner*

⚘

*N*o one ever found their way
who didn't lose their anger.

—*Noah benShea*

⚘

A man should study ever to keep cool.
He makes his inferiors his superiors by heat.

—*Ralph Waldo Emerson*

⚘

*W*hen thou art above measure angry, bethinks thee how
momentary is man's life. Bethinks thee how much more
grievous are the consequences of our anger than the acts
which arouse it. Let this truth be present to thee in the
excitement of anger, that to be moved by passion is not
manly, but that mildness and gentleness, as they are
more human, so also are they more manly.

—*Marcus Aurelius*

$\mathcal{I}$t is very difficult for people to believe the simple fact
that every persecutor was once a victim. Yet it should be
very obvious that someone who was allowed to feel free
and strong from childhood does not have the need
to humiliate another person.

—*Alice Miller*

❧

$\mathcal{T}$he greatest remedy for anger is delay.

—*Marcus Annaens Seneca*

❧

$\mathcal{W}$hen we acknowledge our children's right to want
things, as well as their right to be upset when they can't
have what they want, it can go a long way toward defusing
their anger and the tantrums that occur as a result.

—*Nancy Samalin*

❧

$\mathcal{C}$hildren are intensely invested in getting their way.
They will devote more emotional and intellectual energy
to winning arguments than parents ever will, and are
almost always better rested.

—*Jean Callahan*

❧

$\mathcal{I}$gnoring a child's disrespect is the surest guarantee
that it will continue.

—*Fred G. Gosman*

$\mathcal{W}$herever I look, I see signs of the commandment to honor one's parents and nowhere of a commandment that calls for the respect of a child.

—*Alice Miller*

⬚

$\mathcal{W}$e now recognize that abuse and neglect may be as frequent in nuclear families as love, protection, and commitment are in non-nuclear families.

—*David Elkind*

⬚

$\mathcal{T}$he hearts of small children are delicate organs. A cruel beginning in this world can twist them into curious shapes. The heart of a hurt child can shrink so that forever afterward it is hard and pitted as the seed of a peach. Or, again, the heart of such a child may fester and swell until it is misery to carry within the body, easily chafed and hurt by the most ordinary things.

—*Carson McCullers*

⬚

$\mathcal{T}$hose children who are beaten will in turn give beatings, those who are intimidated will be intimidating, those who are humiliated will impose humiliation, and those whose souls are murdered will murder.

—*Alice Miller*

*T*here's nothing wrong with teenagers
that reasoning with them won't aggravate.

—Anonymous

🌸

*S*chools cannot shut their door and expect a safe "castle"
where outside influences don't enter.

—Carl Bosch

🌸

*W*e may not always see eye to eye, but we can try
to see heart to heart.

—Sam Levenson

🌸

*C*onstant kindness can accomplish much. As the sun
makes ice melt, kindness causes misunderstanding,
mistrust, and hostility to evaporate.

—Albert Schweitzer

🌸

*S*adism is not an infectious disease that strikes a person
all of a sudden. It has a long prehistory in childhood and
always originates in the desperate fantasies of a child
who is searching for a way out of a hopeless situation.

—Alice Miller

SPIRITUALITY

*E*very soul is a melody
which needs renewing.
—*Stéphane Mallarmé*

*P*rayer is a path where there is none.

—*Noah benShea*

❈

*S*et your affection on things above,
not on things on the earth.

—*Bible: Colossians 3:2*

❈

*W*e praise Him, we bless Him, we adore Him, we glorify
Him, and we wonder who is that baritone across the aisle
and that pretty woman on our right who smells of apple
blossoms . . . . We amend our prayers for the spiritual life
with the hope that it will not be too spiritual.

—*John Cheever*

❈

*Z*en . . . does not confuse spirituality with thinking
about God while one is peeling potatoes.
Zen spirituality is just to peel the potatoes.

—*Alan Watts*

❈

*G*od is always in concert; the audience
is not always listening.

—*Noah benShea*

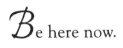

$\mathcal{B}$e here now.

—*Ram Dass*

$\mathcal{P}$ure Spirit, one hundred degrees proof—
that's a drink that only the most hardened
contemplation-guzzlers indulge in.
Bodhisattvas dilute their Nirvana
with equal parts of love and work.

—*Aldous Huxley*

$\mathcal{D}$o not do unto others what you would
not have them do unto you.
The rest is commentary. Go and study.

—*Hillel*

$\mathcal{T}$he reason for religion is not reason.

—*Noah benShea*

$\mathcal{Y}$our soul . . . is a dark forest.
But the trees are of a particular species,
they are genealogical trees.

—*Marcel Proust*

*T*he Soul unto itself
Is an imperial friend—
Or the most agonizing Spy—
An Enemy—could send—

—*Emily Dickinson*

✠

*W*e are what we think.
All that we are arises with our thoughts.
With our thoughts we make the world.
Speak or act with an impure mind,
And trouble will follow you
As the wheel follows the ox that draws the cart.

We are what we think.
All that we are arises with our thoughts.
With our thoughts we make the world.
Speak or act with a pure mind,
And happiness will follow you
As your shadow, unshakable.

—*Buddha*

✠

*W*hy do you hasten to remove anything which hurts
your eye, while if something affects your soul
you postpone the cure until next year?

—*Horace*

*T*he Buddha, the Godhead, resides quite as comfortably
  in the circuits of a digital computer or the gears
  of a cycle transmission as he does at the top
  of a mountain or in the petals of a flower.

—*Robert M. Pirsig*

❧

*Y*ou are the secret of God's secret.
You are the mirror of divine beauty.

—*Rumi*

❧

*T*he natural flights of the human mind are not from
  pleasure to pleasure, but from hope to hope.

—*Samuel Johnson*

❧

*M*ost people sell their souls, and live
  with a good conscience on the proceeds.

—*Logan Pearsall Smith*

❧

*W*e are people with lanterns going in search of a light.

—*Noah benShea*

*T*his soul, or life within us, by no means agrees
with the life outside us.

—*Virginia Woolf*

✠

*A*s in the microcosm so is the macrocosm.
As in the atom, so is the universe.
As in the human body, so is the cosmic body.
As in human mind, so is the cosmic mind.

—*The Vedas*

✠

*G*od has promised those of them who believe
and do deeds of righteousness forgiveness
and a mighty wage.

—*Qur'an*

✠

*M*y soul is my great asset and my great misfortune.

—*D. H. Lawrence*

✠

*T*he logic of worldly success rests on a fallacy:
the strange error that our perfection depends on the
thoughts and opinions and applause of other men!
A weird life it is, indeed, to be living always
in somebody else's imagination, as if that were
the only place in which one could at last become real!

—*Thomas Merton*

*G*od doesn't require us to succeed; God only
    requires that we try.

—*Mother Teresa*

☙

*T*hose who awaken
Never rest in one place.
Like Swans, they rise
And leave the lake.

—*Buddha*

☙

I am the bread of life: he that cometh to me shall never
hunger; and he that believeth on me shall never thirst.

—*Bible: Jesus, in John 6:35*

☙

*N*o matter what you're thinking,
    your thoughts disturb the pond.
Only a quiet pond paints an honest picture.

—*Noah benShea*

☙

*Y*ou don't calm the waters by walking in them.

—*Lao Tzu*

☙

*B*efore you can find God you must lose yourself.

—*Ba'al Shem Tov*

*T*o be inspired by God means to literally breathe the Divine into our being. Slow down. Take a breather. And you'll find yourself inspired.

—*Don Hartsock*

❧

*L*et go of anger.
Let go of pride.
When you are bound by nothing,
You go beyond sorrow.

—*Buddha*

❧

*C*all upon Me in the day of trouble.

—*Bible, Psalms 50:15*

❧

*F*aith sees around corners.

—*Noah benShea*

STRESS, REST, AND
WELL-BEING

$\mathcal{J}$'ve had a lot of problems
in my life and most of
them never happened.

—Mark Twain

*L*earning to relax can be hard work.

—*Noah benShea*

❧

I've tried relaxing, but—I don't know—
I feel more comfortable tense.

—*Hamilton Cartoon*

❧

*M*ost stress is caused by people who overestimate
the importance of their problems.

—*Michael LeBoeuf*

❧

*S*tress is a state of fatigue or frustration brought about
by devotion to a cause, way of life, or relationship
that failed to produce the expected reward.

—*Herbert J. Freudenberger*

❧

*W*hat does not bend breaks.

—*Unknown*

❧

*S*tress is defined as an inability, or the perception that
you are unable, to take control in your life. If you feel in
control—even if you're not but perceive that you are—
you won't feel the stress.

—*Gary Grody*

*U*nless we come apart and rest awhile,
we may just plain come apart.

—*Vance Havner*

❋

*L*oosen your laces.
People with tight shoes wear pressured grins.

—*Noah benShea*

❋

*I*n most incidences, it's not the individual or the job
that causes Burnout. Burnout is the result of a mismatch
between the personality or the goals of the worker and the
job description or the expectations of the workplace.

—*Paul Rosch*

❋

*T*hose who feel a sense of purpose and commitment, who
view change as a challenge instead of threat, aren't
affected by stress in a negative way.

—Success *Magazine*

❋

*R*est is not idleness, and to lie sometimes on the grass
under the trees on a summer's day, listening to the murmur
of the water, or watching the clouds float across the blue
sky, is by no means a waste of time.

—*Lord Averbury*

*T*ake rest; a field that has rested gives a bountiful crop.

—*Ovid*

❧

*I*t is well to lie fallow for a while.

—*Martin F. Tupper*

❧

*R*est awhile and run a mile.

—*Palsgrave*

❧

*R*est and success are fellows.

—*W. G. Benham*

❧

*S*ometimes what we resist doing
is our greatest achievement.

—*Noah benShea*

❧

*T*he bow that's always bent will quickly break.

—*Phaedrus, Fables*

❧

*N*othing in the affairs of men is worthy of great anxiety.

—*Plato*

*I*f you had to define stress, it would not be far off if you said it was the process of living. The process of living is the process of having stress imposed on you and reacting to it.

—*Stanley J. Sarnoff*

❈

*O*n every mountain height is Rest.

—*Johann Wolfgang Von Goethe*

❈

A person who is master of himself can end a sorrow as easily as he can invent a pleasure.

—*Oscar Wilde*

❈

*H*e who cannot change the very fabric of his thought will never be able to change reality.

—*Anwar Sadat*

❈

*I*t's not what you think you are— but what you think, you are.

—*Unknown*

*T*he mind is its own place, and in itself, can make
heaven of Hell, and a hell of Heaven.

—*John Milton*

❦

*W*e are more often frightened than hurt; and we suffer
more from imagination than from reality.

—*Marcus Annaeus Seneca*

❦

*L*aughing is sometimes the best way to cry.

—*Noah benShea*

❦

*P*lease God, don't show me what I can bear.

—*Yiddish proverb*

❦

*T*he only difference between a diamond and a lump
of coal is that the diamond had a little more pressure
put on it.

—*Anonymous*

❦

*I*t takes a real storm in the average person's life
to make him realize how much worrying
he has done over the squalls.

—*Anonymous*

*I*t's not stress that kills us, it is our reaction to it.

—*Hans Selye*

❦

*E*very now and then go away, have a little relaxation,
for when you come back to your work your judgment
will be surer. Go some distance away because then
the work appears smaller and more of it can
be taken in at a glance and a lack of harmony
and proportion is more readily seen.

—*Leonardo Da Vinci*

❦

*S*tepping back from things can give us a closer view.

—*Noah benShea*

TECHNOLOGY

*O*ur Age of Anxiety is, in great part, the result of trying to do today's jobs with yesterday's tools.

—*Marshall McLuhan*

*T*he birth of technology is touted to have been
when our first ancestor picked up a rock as a weapon.
Perhaps. But surely, the mastery of technology is when
the rock was put down. Until we can master the same,
we are victims of our genius, and every
great leap forward is a step back.

—*Noah benShea*

❈

*A*ny sufficiently advanced technology is
indistinguishable from magic.

—*Arthur C. Clarke*

❈

*T*echnology is not in itself opposed to spirituality
and to religion. But it presents a great temptation.

—*Thomas Merton*

❈

*E*verything that can be invented, has been invented.

—*Charles H. Duell (1899)*

❈

*T*he most likely way for the world to be destroyed, most
experts agree, is by accident. That's where we come in;
we're computer professionals. We cause accidents.

—*Nathaniel Borenstein*

$\mathcal{I}$ do not fear computers. I fear lack of them.

—*Isaac Asimov*

❧

$\mathcal{W}$isdom surrounds us.
It is seldom hidden but often overlooked.

—*Noah benShea*

❧

$\mathcal{I}$f the automobile had followed the same development cycle as the computer, a Rolls-Royce would today cost $100, get one million miles to the gallon, and explode once a year, killing everyone inside.

—*Robert X. Cringely*

❧

$\mathcal{H}$ardware: the parts of a computer that can be kicked.

—*Jeff Pesis*

❧

$\mathcal{A}$ computer lets you make more mistakes faster than any invention in human history—with the possible exceptions of handguns and tequila.

—*Mitch Ratliffe*

*T*echnological progress has merely provided us
with more efficient means for going backwards.

—*Aldous Huxley*

ᛘ

*T*he world is very different now. For man holds
in his mortal hands the power to abolish all forms
of human poverty, and all forms of human life.

—*John F. Kennedy*

ᛘ

*W*e can drown in our technology. The fog
of information can drive out knowledge.

—*Daniel Boorstin*

ᛘ

*I*t is only by the rational use of technology—to control
and guide what technology is doing—that we can keep
any hopes of a social life more desirable than our own,
or in fact of a social life which is not
appalling to imagine.

—*C. P. Snow*

ᛘ

*O*ur technology has already outstripped
our ability to control it.

—*General Omar Bradley*

$\mathcal{T}$echnology . . . is a queer thing. It brings you great gifts
with one hand, and it stabs you in the back with the other.
—*C. P. Snow*

❈

$\mathcal{I}$f we had a reliable way to label our toys good and bad,
it would be easy to regulate technology wisely.
But we can rarely see far enough ahead to know
which road leads to damnation.
—*Freeman Dyson*

❈

$\mathcal{T}$he science of today is the technology of tomorrow.
—*Edward Teller*

❈

$\mathcal{T}$echnology feeds on itself. Technology makes
more technology possible.
—*Alvin Toffler*

❈

$\mathcal{T}$echnology makes it possible for people to gain control
over everything, except over technology.
—*John Tudor*

*I*t has become appallingly obvious that our technology
has exceeded our humanity.

—*Albert Einstein*

❧

*O*urs is a world of nuclear giants and ethical infants.
If we continue to develop our technology without wisdom
or prudence, our servant may prove to be our executioner.

—*General Omar Bradley*

❧

*I*n life
what we catch
isn't always what we bait our hook for.

—*Noah benShea*

TESTING 24

*T*each the students–
not the test.

—*Anonymous*

*L*ife is not a test, but we are all tested.
So pay attention and take notes.

—*Noah benShea*

❧

A student by definition doesn't know
what he or she doesn't know.

—*Michael Gorman*

❧

A university professor set an examination question in
which he asked what is the difference between ignorance
and apathy. The professor had to give an A+ to a student
who answered: I don't know and I don't care.

—*Richard Pratt, Pacific Computer Weekly, 20 July 1990*

❧

*E*ducation is the state-controlled manufacture of echoes.

—*Norman Douglas*

❧

*E*xperience is not what happens to you.
It is what you do with what happens to you.

—*Aldous Huxley*

*G*od made the Idiot for practice, and then
He made the School Board.

—*Mark Twain*

❈

*I*t is a miracle that curiosity survives formal education.
The only thing that interferes with my learning
is my education.

—*Albert Einstein*

❈

*Y*ou're aware the boy failed my grade school
math class, I take it?

—*Karl Arbeiter (former teacher of Albert Einstein)*

❈

*S*ometimes it's useful to know how large your zero is.

—*Anonymous*

❈

*A*n intelligence test sometimes shows a man how smart
he would have been not to have taken it.

—*Laurence J. Peter*

❈

*T*he greatest obstacle to discovery is not ignorance—
it is the illusion of knowledge.

—*Daniel J. Boorstin*

Knowledge must come through action; you can have no test which is not fanciful, save by trial.

—*Sophocles*

⚜

This life is a test. It is only a test. Had this been an actual life, you would have received further instructions as to what to do and where to go.

—*Unknown*

⚜

We are given children to test us and make us more spiritual.

—George F. Will

⚜

If someone offers to furnish a sure test, ask what the test was which made the sure test sure.

—*Unknown*

⚜

Everything you've learned in school as "obvious" becomes less and less obvious as you begin to study the universe. For example, there are no solids in the universe. There's not even a suggestion of a solid. There are no absolute continuums. There are no surfaces. There are no straight lines.

—R. Buckminster Fuller

*T*o be ignorant of one's ignorance
is the malady of the ignorant.

—*A. B. Alcott*

❦

*S*tudies serve for delight, for ornament, and for ability.

—*Francis Bacon*

❦

*S*triving for excellence motivates you;
striving for perfection is demoralizing.

—*Harriet Braiker*

❦

*S*uccess, or failure, very often arrives on wings
that seem mysterious to us.

—*Marcus Bach*

❦

*O*ne's best success comes after their greatest
disappointments.

—*Henry Ward Beecher*

❦

*S*uccess isn't always to the swift.
Going slowly can be its own success.

—*Noah benShea*

*T*he road to success runs uphill.

—*Willie Davis*

❧

*T*o give your best is to receive the best.

—*Raymond Holliwell*

❧

*S*uccessful people are not gifted; they just work hard, then succeed on purpose.

—*G. K. Nielson*

❧

*T*he most important of my discoveries has been suggested to me by my failures.

—*Sir Humphrey Davy*

❧

*Y*ou always pass failure on the way to success.

—*Mickey Rooney*

❧

*G*ood people are good because they've come to wisdom through failure.

—*William Saroyan*

*F*ailure to prepare is preparing to fail.

—*Unknown*

❧

*T*he only real failure in life is one not learned from.

—*Anthony J. D'Angelo*

❧

*L*ack of willpower has caused more failure than lack of intelligence or ability.

—*Flower A. Newhouse*

❧

*W*hen defeat overtakes a man, the easiest and most logical thing to do is to quit. That is exactly what the majority of men do.

—*Napolean Hill*

❧

*S*ometimes a noble failure serves the world as faithfully as a distinguished success.

—*Edward Dowden*

*A*n old puzzle asks how a barometer can be used to measure the height of a building. Answers range from dropping the instrument from the top and measuring the time of its fall to giving it to the building's superintendent in return for a look at the plans. A modern version of the puzzle asks how a personal computer can balance a checkbook. An elegant solution is to sell the machine and deposit the money.

—*Jon Bentley*, More Programming Pearls

TIME AND RESOURCES MANAGEMENT

25

*T*he secret of getting
ahead is getting started.

—*Mark Twain*

*A*ll management begins with self-management.

—*Noah benShea*

❧

*F*orewarned, forearmed; to be prepared
is half the victory.

—*Miguel de Cervantes*, Don Quixote

❧

*O*ne must prepare himself today for what he wishes
to be tomorrow. Preparedness is better than hope.

—*Alexis Lawrence Romanoff*

❧

*O*ne of these days is none of these days.

—*H. C. Bohn*

❧

*D*elays have dangerous ends.

—*Shakespeare, I Henry VI*

❧

*Y*ou manage things . . . you lead people.

—*Jim Clemmer*

*I*ncreasingly, the people who are the most effective
are those who essentially are both managers and leaders.
—*David Thomas*

❧

*T*he less one has to do, the less time one finds to do it in.
—*Lord Chesterfield*

❧

*W*e always have time for the things we put first.
—*Unknown*

❧

*T*ime is an orchard.
Every moment is ripe with opportunity.
—*Noah benShea*

❧

*W*e can no more afford to spend major time on minor
things than we can to spend minor time on major things.
—*Jim Rohn*

❧

*I*t is not time which needs to be managed; it is ourselves.
—*Gillian Butler and Tony Hope*

I hated every minute of training, but I said,
"Don't quit." Suffer now and live
the rest of your life as a champion.

—*Muhammad Ali*

❈

*R*emember, it wasn't raining when Noah built the ark.

—*Howard Ruff*

❈

*T*ime is the scarcest resource and unless it is managed
nothing else can be managed.

—*Peter Drucker*

❈

*T*ime does not wait for us to learn our lesson
before it moves us on to the next.

—*Noah benShea*

❈

*Y*esterday is gone. Tomorrow has not yet come.
We have only today. Let us begin.

—*Mother Teresa*

26

WOMEN IN EDUCATION

*T*here is no female mind.
The brain is not an organ
of sex. Might as well speak
of a female liver.

—*Charlotte Perkins Gillman*

*M*y mother used to always say,
"If you want to give God a good laugh
tell Her your plans."

—*Noah benShea*

❧

*W*e haven't come a long way, we've come a short way.
If we hadn't come a short way, no one
would be calling us "baby."

—*Elizabeth Janeway*

❧

*T*o be meek, patient, tactful, modest, honorable, brave, is
not to be either manly or womanly; it is to be humane.

—*Jane Harrison*

❧

*R*emember, Ginger Rogers did everything Fred Astaire
did, but she did it backwards and in high heels.

—*Faith Whittlesey*

❧

*F*eminism is the radical notion that women are people.

—*Cheris Kramare and Paula Treichler*

❧

*M*en, their rights, and nothing more;
women, their rights, and nothing less.

—*Susan B. Anthony and Elizabeth Cady Stanton*

$\mathcal{U}$nfortunately, sometimes people don't
hear you until you scream.

—*Stefanie Powers*

🌼

$\mathcal{S}$ince when do we have to agree with people
to defend them from injustice?

—*Lillian Hellman*

🌼

$\mathcal{T}$here are many ways to be free. One of them is
to transcend reality by imagination, as I try to do.

—*Anaïs Nin*

🌼

$\mathcal{W}$omen must understand that simply attacking or
hating men is just another form of disempowerment.
A woman has to realize that when she makes
a man crawl it doesn't give her power.

—*Tori Amos*

🌼

$\mathcal{I}$f you're going to hold someone down you're going
to have to hold on by the other end of the chain.
You are confined by your own repression.

—*Toni Morrison*

I don't mind how much my ministers talk—
as long as they do what I say.

—*Margaret Thatcher*

❧

*I*n the end antiblack, antifemale, and all forms
of discrimination are equivalent to the same thing—
antihumanism.

—*Shirley Chisholm*

❧

*S*ometimes I feel discriminated against, but it does not
make me angry. It merely astonishes me. How can they
deny themselves the pleasure of my company?
It's beyond me.

—*Zora Neale Hurston*

❧

*B*ecause I am a woman, I must make unusual efforts to
succeed. If I fail, no one will say, "She doesn't have what it
takes." They will say, "Women don't have what it takes."

—*Clare Boothe Luce*

❧

*W*omen are repeatedly accused of taking things
personally. I cannot see any other honest way
of taking them.

—*Marya Mannes*

*I*f society will not allow a woman's free development,
then society must be remodeled.

—*Elizabeth Blackwell*

❧

*W*oman's discontent increases in exact proportion
to her development.

—*Elizabeth Cady Stanton*

❧

I never expect men to give us liberty. No, women,
we are not worth it until we take it.

—*Voltairine de Cleyre*

❧

*O*ur struggle today is not to have a female Einstein get
appointed as an assistant professor. It is for a woman
schlemiel to get as quickly promoted
as a male schlemiel.

—*Bella Abzug*

❧

*T*he Rubicons which women must cross,
the sex barriers which they must breach,
are ultimately those that exist in their own minds.

—*Freda Adler*

❧

*I*f you can't be a good example, then you'll just
have to be a horrible warning.

—*Catherine Aird*

※

I'm just a person trapped inside a woman's body.

—*Elayne Boosler*

※

*T*he true aim of female education should be, not a
development of one or two, but all the faculties of the
human soul, because no perfect womanhood is
developed by imperfect culture.

—*Frances Watkins Harper*

※

*T*he only jobs for which no man is qualified are human
incubator and wet nurse. Likewise, the only job for which
no woman is or can be qualified is sperm donor.

—*Wilma Scott Heide*

※

*T*he problem is that when I go around and speak on
campuses, I still don't get young men standing up
and saying, "How can I combine career and family?"

—*Gertrude Stein*

Speak truth to power.

—*Anonymous*

🌷

There is more difference within the sexes than between them.

—*Ivy Compton-Burnett*

END WORD

A quotation at the right
moment is like bread in
a famine.

—*The Talmud*